**New Directions for
Adult and Continuing
Education**

Susan Imel
Jovita M. Ross-Gordon
COEDITORS-IN-CHIEF

Popular Culture and Entertainment Media in Adult Education

Elizabeth J. Tisdell,
Patricia M. Thompson
EDITORS

Number 115 • Fall 2007
Jossey-Bass
San Francisco

POPULAR CULTURE AND ENTERTAINMENT MEDIA IN ADULT EDUCATION
Elizabeth J. Tisdell, Patricia M. Thompson (eds.)
New Directions for Adult and Continuing Education, no. 115
Susan Imel, Jovita M. Ross-Gordon, Coeditors-in-Chief

Microfilm copies of issues and articles are available in 16mm and 35mm, as well as microfiche in 105mm, through University Microfilms Inc., 300 North Zeeb Road, Ann Arbor, Michigan 48106-1346.

NEW DIRECTIONS FOR ADULT AND CONTINUING EDUCATION (ISSN 1052-2891, electronic ISSN 1536-0717) is part of The Jossey-Bass Higher and Adult Education Series and is published quarterly by Wiley Subscription Services, Inc., A Wiley Company, at Jossey-Bass, 989 Market Street, San Francisco, California 94103-1741. Periodicals Postage Paid at San Francisco, California, and at additional mailing offices. POSTMASTER: Send address changes to New Directions for Adult and Continuing Education, Jossey-Bass, 989 Market Street, San Francisco, California 94103-1741.

New Directions for Adult and Continuing Education is indexed in CIJE: Current Index to Journals in Education (ERIC); Contents Pages in Education (T&F); ERIC Database (Education Resources Information Center; Higher Education Abstracts (Claremont Graduate University); and Sociological Abstracts (CSA/CIG).

SUBSCRIPTIONS cost $85.00 for individuals and $209.00 for institutions, agencies, and libraries.

EDITORIAL CORRESPONDENCE should be sent to the Coeditors-in-Chief, Susan Imel, ERIC/ACVE, 1900 Kenny Road, Columbus, Ohio 43210-1090, e-mail: imel.l@osu.edu; or Jovita M. Ross-Gordon, Southwest Texas State University, EAPS Dept., 601 University Drive, San Marcos, TX 78666.

Cover photograph by Jack Hollingsworth@Photodisc

Wiley Bicentennial Logo: Richard J. Pacifico

www.josseybass.com

CONTENTS

EDITORS' NOTES

Popular culture and entertainment media have an enormous influence on all of us. We are constantly bombarded with messages through media such as billboards, advertisements, movies, popular music, television shows, and radio. These messages affect who we are and how we think both about ourselves and about other people. Thus, popular culture is a presently unexplored area of adult education that has far more power to educate or "miseducate" than all adult education programs combined because of the sheer numbers it reaches. This volume attempts to fill that gap in the field; it examines how educators of adults might draw on popular culture in their work.

We don't have to think hard to recognize the influences of popular culture. For example, most North Americans know that Ward and June Cleaver of *Leave It to Beaver* fame are seen as icons of 1950s life in middle-class white America. Many Saturday morning errand runners recognize Click and Clack, the Tappit Brothers, as the funny guys with the Boston accents who tell people what's wrong with their cars on the radio show *Car Talk*. Most across the English-speaking world are familiar with Homer, Marge (with the famous blue beehive hair-do), and Bart from the satirical animated TV show *The Simpsons,* which pokes fun at everyone on all sides of an issue. Finally, the still popular 1980s through 1990s *Cosby Show,* which featured a professional-class black family, continues to entertain people across the world through syndicated TV.

Media such as film and television have also created their own insider language; many famous lines from movies or television are in common use and often bring a smile of recognition about their origins. For example, most recognize the expression "Not that there's anything wrong with that" as a line from the *Seinfeld* sitcom, and they know that the line "Frankly, my dear, I don't give a damn" was Rhett Butler's stinging rebuke to Scarlet O'Hara in the movie *Gone with the Wind*. Similarly, "This isn't Kansas anymore" has come to refer to changing times. Its use takes many of us back to our childhoods, when we huddled around the family TV set watching Dorothy and her friends in *The Wizard of Oz* battle the Wicked Witch, while seeking out the wizard to help her find her way back home.

We have all been dually entertained and informed by one or more of these icons of popular culture. Many of these fictional characters have made us laugh, sometimes at ourselves; some have even taught us important

DISCOVER SOMETHING GREAT

NEW DIRECTIONS FOR ADULT AND CONTINUING EDUCATION, no. 115, Fall 2007 © 2007 Wiley Periodicals, Inc.
Published online in Wiley InterScience (www.interscience.wiley.com) • DOI: 10.1002/ace.261

lessons about life. Think about *The Wizard of Oz*. Dorothy learns that home is inside herself; the Scarecrow learns that he is smart; and all of us learned that the wizard is inside each of us. But, along with these overt messages, popular culture and entertainment media contain covert messages that we might not think much about. For example, in the shows mentioned above, with the exception of *The Cosby Show*, the main characters are white and predominantly male, tend to have traditional gender and relational arrangements, and disproportionately represent the relatively moneyed class.

Only with a critical lens do we begin to notice these messages. Unfortunately, however, most of the time, we check our critical minds at the door as we enter the TV room or movie theater. We enjoy entertainment media because they are fun and aesthetically pleasing; they can even provide a social experience. Why spoil the party with critical analysis? It is not our intention here to encourage educators to disregard the entertainment value of media. But we do want to provide educators with the tools necessary to be critical consumers of media so that they can encourage learners to be such consumers also. Adults need to recognize the education and miseducation that occur on a daily basis, at both a conscious and unconscious level, through popular culture and entertainment media.

Popular culture surrounds us, and it surrounds those we teach in adult education settings. Even adults who do not spend much time in front of a television screen are familiar with the characters and themes of popular shows. Many who do not know a thing about football tune in every year to watch the commercials during the Super Bowl. Even if one never turns on a television or goes to a movie, entertainment media are mass-marketed through other channels such as apparel, toys and games, snack foods and cereals. It is virtually impossible to escape their presence and influence. However, it is possible to be an active participant with the media, consciously creating knowledge and understanding, rather than simply being a passive recipient of media messages.

In the chapters that follow, we share several examples of the interplay between popular culture and entertainment media in adult and continuing education settings. The first and last chapters are written by us as editors. In Chapter One, to set the stage and provide a theoretical framework for integrating popular culture and adult and continuing education, Elizabeth J. Tisdell provides a theoretical overview and presents the current literature on the use of popular culture and entertainment in both education and the development of critical media literacy.

In Chapter Two, Talmadge C. Guy discusses the powerful influence that popular culture and entertainment media have on adults. He emphasizes the importance of developing critical media-literacy skills and provides examples from his practice as a university professor and adult educator; these examples focus on using popular culture to highlight societal perceptions of race, gender, and social class. In Chapter Three, Heather Stuckey and Kelly

Kring continue to encourage the development of critical media-literacy skills by discussing popular movies and semiotics and by sharing their experiences as both teacher and learner in the graduate classroom.

Chapter Four connects the college classroom with the real world of educators as they learn about the educational value of hip hop. Mary Stone Hanley provides rich examples of student learning and teacher transformation as she works toward bridging the generational gap between teachers and youth immersed in hip hop culture. Although she acknowledges the criticisms of hip hop, she constructs a compelling argument for recognizing hip hop as a tool for culturally relevant instruction and as a way to connect with students and youth who are often disenfranchised and not engaged by traditional educational practices.

In Chapter Five, Maxwell A. Fink and Deborah C. Foote share their knowledge about and passion for the popular animated show *The Simpsons*. They both use *The Simpsons* in their teaching practice to encourage Gen X and Gen Y students to critically assess societal norms and to challenge their understandings of themselves and others in Humanities classes. Because Fink and Foote work in different contexts and teach different humanities subjects, this chapter provides an excellent illustration of how popular culture can be integrated into multidisciplinary curricula.

Barbara P. Heuer challenges traditional views of literacy and literacy education in Chapter Six by encouraging educators to recognize the informal learning that takes place on a daily basis through individuals' interaction with popular culture and entertainment media. She encourages literacy educators to expand their understanding of literacy to include critical media literacy. Finally, she provides examples of how she integrates popular culture into her educational practice with literacy educators and students.

In Chapter Seven, Robin Redmon Wright takes us back in time and "across the pond" to introduce us to the show *The Avengers*, which was popular in Britain in the 1960s. She shares poignant examples of the transformational and emancipatory power of the media through the reflections of women whose lives were affected by the self-reliant, well-educated character of Dr. Catherine Gale, an anomaly in postwar British culture.

Chapter Eight introduces another aspect of popular culture: its use in cultural resistance. Jennifer A. Sandlin informs us about the activity of "culture jamming" and introduces us to Adbusters and Reverend Billy's Church of Stop Shopping. These groups challenge the advertisement-oriented, consumerist culture through the use of alternative spaces such as internet sites. Sandlin presents a compelling argument for educators of adults to consider culture jamming as a form of education, especially in the areas of social justice and the politics of consumption.

In Chapter Nine, the final chapter, Patricia M. Thompson summarizes the themes presented throughout the volume and encourages adult educators to incorporate critical media literacy into their teaching practices. In addition, this chapter briefly presents some considerations for the future as alternative spaces and forms of entertainment media begin to emerge.

We'd like to thank all the authors for their work and insights. We'd also especially like to thank Michele Mont for editing and proofreading each chapter.

Elizabeth J. Tisdell
Patricia M. Thompson
Editors

ELIZABETH J. TISDELL is associate professor and coordinator of the Adult Education Doctoral Program at the Pennsylvania State University, Harrisburg.

PATRICIA M. THOMPSON is a doctoral student in adult education at the Pennsylvania State University, Harrisburg, and currently works as the editorial associate for the Adult Education Quarterly.

New Directions for Adult and Continuing Education • DOI: 10.1002/ace

1

This chapter introduces the volume, provides an overview of the theory and literature on popular culture and critical media literacy in education, and discusses ways to use popular culture in adult education.

Popular Culture and Critical Media Literacy in Adult Education: Theory and Practice

Elizabeth J. Tisdell

I love a good story. I love seeing great movies and reading provocative novels, especially those relatively new and "hot" books that make me think in new ways about things I'm interested in. As an academic, I seldom have time to see movies or read novels, except during breaks. So I spent the first two days of the semester break in December 2003 reading the very hot and extremely provocative book *The Da Vinci Code* by Dan Brown (2003). I was riveted! The book is clearly a page-turner and took me to places in Paris and London that I'd either been to before or would love to visit. In this fictional story, the main characters uncover a centuries-old conspiracy in the Catholic Church concealing that Jesus had been married to Mary Magdalene and that they had had a child. Thus, Mary Magdalene herself was actually the Holy Grail, the vessel or "cup" that carried the child. The novel provides an entertaining combination of thrill and mystery as the main characters decipher the messages of the Da Vinci code to uncover the conspiracy. The author leaves the reader hanging at the end of every chapter, so I simply had to keep turning the pages!

Needless to say, the book caused an uproar both in Christian religious circles and in more secular spheres as well. It clearly made people think and had people talking. Some said that Brown overstepped bounds in mixing religious history and fiction (Noonan, 2006). Others (both Christian and non-Christian) suggested that the book gave people insight into the way power relations might shape how history is written, how what is taught as

NEW DIRECTIONS FOR ADULT AND CONTINUING EDUCATION, no. 115, Fall 2007 © 2007 Wiley Periodicals, Inc.
Published online in Wiley InterScience (www.interscience.wiley.com) • DOI: 10.1002/ace.262

historical truth by a particular religious tradition might have been partially propagated by the religious hierarchy of that tradition to serve its own interests. As a result of the book's popularity and the uproar it caused, many pastors felt the need to preach on the *The Da Vinci Code* in order to clarify the difference between fiction and historical evidence. No matter what one's personal opinion about it, *The Da Vinci Code* clearly has had a strong influence on recent dialogues about religious history and, according to Gary Hoppenstand (2005), the book "now ranks as the best-selling novel of all time" and "has had more booklength studies written about it than has any other work of fiction published since World War II" (p. 794).

The stir that *The Da Vinci Code,* which also eventually became a movie, caused is but one example of the role that popular culture can play in society. Popular culture in all its forms is everywhere. It is most obviously present in media, such as movies, television, radio, music, comic books, advertisements, billboards, magazines, and popular fiction. Given that it's ubiquitous, it is a "public pedagogy" (Giroux, 2004) that has far more power to educate or "miseducate" than the many formal and nonformal forms of adult education that scholars have written about and researched. The purpose of this volume is to directly consider how educators of adults can and do draw on popular culture in many different settings as an educational tool. This chapter sets the context by providing an overview of some of the literature on popular culture and media literacy in adult education and on the development of critical media literacy. In addition, it highlights the contributions each of the chapters makes and explains how the book is organized.

The Literature on Popular Culture in Adult Education

Popular culture has been given relatively little attention in the field of adult education thus far. This is somewhat surprising as the field includes so much theorizing and practical discussion about experiential and informal learning. Further, quite a bit has been written about the use of popular culture and entertainment media in other disciplines: in cultural and media studies, in the K–12 arena, and among those who write about the importance of developing critical media literacy. Critical media literacy is generally concerned with "helping students experience the pleasures of popular culture while simultaneously uncovering the practices that work to silence or disempower them as readers, viewers, and learners" (Alvermann and Hagood, 2000, p. 194). In essence, it's about helping students to learn to read the world as well as the word (Freire, 1971)—in this case, how the world of the media and popular culture can both resist and reinforce the interests of the dominant culture. Much literature in adult education is concerned with challenging and resisting the dominant culture and with teaching people to read the world. Further, in the area of media and cultural studies, a number of research pieces focus on how adults construct their identities in light of popular culture (for example, Hall, 2001; Radway, 1984; Richards, 2005). Given the natural connection between adult education and critical media literacy, it is curious that discussions about teaching people to read the world of media and popular culture are so limited.

Though the literature on popular culture and media analysis specifically in adult education is scant, a small base does exist. In the mid-1980s, Stephen Brookfield (1986) wrote about the importance of developing media literacy in adult education because of the bias in television programming and production. In the late 1980s, Robert Graham (1989) discussed the importance of media literacy in analyzing both women's romance fiction and the role of power relations in shaping the content of television news programs. The fact that Brookfield is originally from England and Graham is Canadian might explain why they were among the first in the field to write about media literacy; as David Considine (2002) observes, the United States has lagged far behind Australia, the United Kingdom, and Canada in developing approaches to critical media literacy.

To a large extent, our colleagues "across the pond" in the United Kingdom have been major contributors to more recent discussions as well. Nod Miller, in a paper presented at the 1999 Adult Education Research Conference, described the contributions of popular culture to the field by drawing on the sitcom *Seinfeld*. More recently, Christine Jarvis (2005) presented an excellent critique of the television show *Buffy the Vampire Slayer* from a feminist perspective, specifically examining its representation not only of formal education but of self-directed adult learning. Paul Armstrong (2005b) has also done a fascinating analysis of the role of the television show *The Simpsons* as political commentary and has discussed the use of satire as critical pedagogy (Armstrong, 2005a).

The United States is lagging behind, but some American scholars have begun to write about popular culture and adult education. Though not specifically identified with the field of adult education, but widely cited by adult educators, the always-on-the-cutting-edge black feminist scholar bell hooks (1994, 1996) has discussed the influence of popular culture and the importance of teaching people to read cultural images from a race, class, and gender perspective. In 2004 Talmadge Guy introduced hip hop to adult education, and Jennifer Sandlin (2005) examined consumer education of adults from a cultural-studies perspective and discussed the implications for a critical pedagogy of consumer education. In addition, Patricia M. Thompson and I have done a large mixed-methods study of the consumption of entertainment media by 215 U.S. adult educators (made up of professors and their graduate students). We examined how entertainment media affect their thinking about group identities based on race, gender, and sexual orientation and how they draw on the media in their teaching and learning. We found that adult educators are large consumers of popular culture as a source of pleasure (Tisdell and Thompson, 2007). The fifteen qualitative interviews indicated that the participants' use of media also helped them find alternative narratives for themselves; expanded thinking about "others" of a different race, gender, or sexual orientation; and furthered interaction and the analysis of social relations both in their own lives and in their teaching. Thus, although the literature base is limited, it appears that adult educators are consumers of popular culture, and they use it to some degree in their teaching. In this volume, several adult educators give voice to the practical aspects of doing so.

Popular Culture and Critical Media Literacy Theory

Popular culture is ubiquitous in society in its multiple forms and influences. All of us are affected by it as we saw in the discussion above of just one popular novel/film, *The Da Vinci Code.* In the case of books and movies, people generally have to intentionally seek out a novel or film. Yet we can be unintentional consumers of popular culture as well, through just passing by billboards and seeing advertisements or from simply being present in our homes when the television is on (even if our spouse, partner, or kids turned it on). For good or for ill, we are constantly being bombarded by messages that affect who we are and how we think, whether we are conscious of those messages or not.

Theories about critical media literacy tend to center on the unconscious effects of popular culture and media influences and on ways of educating for increased consciousness. As Nadine Dolby (2003) observes, many from both the political left and the right have written about the influence of popular culture. Those from the right often decry its evils from the perspective of sexual morality or violence. Those on the left tend to be concerned about the power of creators of the dominant culture to unconsciously lull us into submission to their own interests (Dimitriades and McCarthy, 2000). This was Frankfurt School critical theorist Theodor Adorno's (1991) concern in many of his writings from the mid-1940s to the late 1960s, when he died. He argued that the culture industry was a tool of the dominant culture to subjugate the masses through unconscious means; the more that people are passive consumers of it and do not consciously think about its influence, the more they might fall prey to its unconscious messages. Many who write about critical media literacy and the importance of teaching people to read the world are basing their thought on the pioneering work of Adorno.

Alvermann and Hagood (2000) summarize four threads that run through some of the current theoretical influences and thinking about critical media literacy. In particular, they point out that authors' definitions of critical media literacy depend on their theoretical perspectives and on the primary discipline that informs their work. The first thread highlights the notion of pleasure and focuses on people's ability to reflect on the pleasures associated with being either creators or consumers of media (for example, movie or television viewers or video-game participants). A second thread is from cultural studies and focuses on how media reproduce or resist the dominant culture (Luke, 1999). A third thread is more postmodern than the others; it emphasizes how individuals and groups construct meaning differently depending on their interests, their positionality (their gender, race, class, sexual orientation) relative to the dominant culture, and the historical and social context. Finally, those coming from feminist educational perspectives highlight how media produces gendered and other group-based identities through power relations that students can either use or resist. Educators can use all these perspectives to find ways of drawing on popular culture in their teaching and to develop critical media-literacy skills; their students can use these skills to make active, conscious choices to resist or draw on cultural images in the ongoing construction of their own identities (Buckingham, 2003).

These theoretical threads overlap considerably, and elements from each of them are important. Pleasure is a primary reason people are active consumers of popular culture. It was the primary reason I read *The Da Vinci Code* and the motivation for most people to see particular movies or to tune into their favorite TV shows. Critical media scholars note that because of the pleasure element it is unrealistic to expect people *not* to be consumers of popular culture. Rather, from an educational and media-literacy perspective, it's important to teach people to analyze popular culture's unconscious messages (Hamston, 2002). Henry Giroux (2004) goes even further and argues that educators have a responsibility to do so because popular culture is a mass-produced form of public pedagogy. The three other theoretical strands that Alvermann and Hagood discuss are based on cultural studies and on postmodern and feminist perspectives rather than on pleasure. They collectively highlight how power relations between and among groups inform constructions of media, as well as the ability of individuals to produce their own meaning while still being affected by these power relations between dominant and oppressed groups.

In summarizing the thoughts of numerous critical media scholars, Tara Yosso (2002) offers a helpful framework for both the theory and practice of critical media literacy. She emphasizes that critical media-literacy scholars generally make the following assumptions about entertainment media, particularly in helping students to learn to analyze media: the media are controlled and driven by money; media images are social constructions based on interacting influences on directors, actors, and other media makers; media makers bring their own experience with them in their construction of characters, including their perceptions of race, gender, and class, and those constructions affect how characters are portrayed; consumers of media make their own meaning of media portrayals in light of their own background and experiences and are not strictly passive recipients of media; unlike print media, entertainment media such as movies and television are a combination of moving visuals, sounds, and words that combine in facilitating meaning; it is possible to acquire multiple literacies in becoming media literate, and acquiring these multiple literacies is part of the purpose of education.

In analyzing entertainment media, most authors note that the media tend to reinforce the images and values of the dominant culture. As Scott Coltrane and Melinda Messineo (2000) note, "Media images provide a diffuse confirmation of one's world view, promote acceptance of current social arrangements and reassure people that things are the way they ought to be" (p. 364). But when some entertainment media, overtly or covertly, deal with current social issues regarding race, class, gender, or sexual orientation, they, in some ways, challenge the dominant culture and, in other ways, reproduce it. For example, many movies filmed in the United States (and often broadcast internationally) have overtly dealt with race/ethnic relations or interracial romantic relationships, or they center on women in powerful roles. Many feature main characters who are openly gay or lesbian and portray them as happy and as well adjusted as their heterosexual peers. However, these portrayals often appeal to the dominant culture in that they reinforce that culture's notion of class or other relations. For example, *Will & Grace* focuses on the relationship between a gay man and a straight woman and not on Will's relationships with other gay men (Quimby, 2005); many of the lesbians portrayed on television shows are thin, with long hair, and conform to dominant-culture notions of feminine beauty. Thus such shows may bring visibility to social identities based on sexual orientation, race, class, and gender and may challenge dominant social relations to some extent, but they also reinforce dominant social relations at the same time. As David Buckingham (2003) suggests, media makers dance the dance between their own politics and the funding sources and politics that will keep shows on the air. Exploring the intersection of these issues and the politics involved is part of critical media literacy.

Examples from Practice: The Book's Organization

Most of the literature on critical media literacy has focused on youth education. A few studies have focused on how direct teaching of critical media literacy through analysis of film affects the ways traditional-age college students construct meaning and the identities of themselves and others. This literature includes Nancy Pauly's (2003) study of preservice elementary teachers, Yosso's (2002) study of Latino community college students in the United States, and Ali Nihat Eken's (2002) study of how analysis of popular film at a university in Turkey affects the critical-thinking skills of his students. Such studies do begin to help us understand how educators have used critical media literacy in practice and how it works. The authors in this volume make a large contribution of their own in this regard, particularly as they describe ways to draw on popular culture to facilitate the development of critical media literacy with adult learners.

As mentioned previously, in spite of relatively limited discussion in the adult education field, in our study of educators of adults (Tisdell and Thompson, 2007), we found that they do draw on popular culture and multiple forms of media in their teaching. This opening chapter provides a foundation in the primary theoretical influences and intents of critical media literacy, and the closing chapter by Patricia Thompson provides a summary of the main themes of this volume. As discussed in the Editors' Notes, the chapters in between are rich descriptions of how the authors draw on particular forms of popular culture in specific adult education contexts.

Chapters Two through Five deal with the use of different aspects of popular culture with adult learners in various types of higher education settings. In Chapter Two, Talmadge Guy discusses how popular culture influences people's thinking about group-based identities and how he uses popular culture to deal with diversity and equity issues in his classes. In Chapter Three, Heather Stuckey and Kelly Kring discuss their own experiences as a teacher and a learner in a class that used popular film and semiotics to develop critical media literacy in graduate education students who were themselves either classroom teachers or educators of adults. Mary Hanley, in Chapter Four, discusses how she uses hip hop with teacher educators as a way of helping them learn about culturally responsive education and the importance of drawing on learners' creative expression. Then, Maxwell Fink and Deborah Foote in Chapter Five describe using the popular animated show *The Simpsons* with undergraduate humanities students who are primarily members of Gen X and Gen Y as a way to teach humanities themes and to help the students analyze the influence of the media in their own lives.

Chapters Six through Eight deal with adult education in less formal venues. Barbara Heuer in Chapter Six discusses how to use aspects of popular culture with adult-literacy workers in professional-development workshops. Robin Redmon Wright in Chapter Seven discusses how British women who watched the popular 1960s British television show *The Avengers* drew on the positive influence of the strong and powerful female image of the lead character, Cathy Gale, to construct their own identities as powerful women. Finally, in Chapter Eight, Jennifer Sandlin discusses how popular culture can be used as a tool for cultural resistance, specifically in anticonsumption activities. All these authors highlight how popular culture can be a vehicle of cultural reproduction and cultural resistance at the same time.

Conclusions and Implications for Practice

Popular culture has an important role to play in adult education as a vehicle of critical media literacy. I know that when I teach about gender and diversity issues, students learn far more from analyzing portrayals of characters in television and film as an initial assignment than they do from initially reading high theory about cultural reproduction and resistance. Further, they begin to learn to read the media and to understand the powerful influence the media have both in their own lives and in the lives of those they teach.

Using popular culture can also serve as a bridge by drawing on everyday experiences of the pleasures and influences of media and connecting those experiences to theory. Just as I was riveted by the pleasure, adventure, and mystery of the popular novel and movie *The Da Vinci Code*, students can enter the world of theory through experiences with popular culture that are equally riveting to them. In so doing, they begin to understand the strong influence of popular culture in new ways as they develop their own critical media literacy. Often the association with popular culture facilitates deep theoretical understanding and the discovery that theory is both fascinating and applicable to practice. Just like popular culture, sometimes it's even fun!

References

Adorno, T. W. *The Culture Industry: Selected Essays on Mass Culture.* (J. M. Bernstein, trans.). London: Routledge, 1991.

Alvermann, D. E., and Hagood, M. C. "Critical Media Literacy: Research, Theory, and Practice in 'New Times.'" *Journal of Educational Research,* 2000, 93(3), 193–205.

Armstrong, P. "Satire as Critical Pedagogy." In J. Caldwell and others (eds.), *What a Difference a Pedagogy Makes: Researching Lifelong Learning and Teaching.* Conference Proceedings, vol. 1. Stirling, Scotland: Centre for Research in Lifelong Learning, University of Stirling, 2005a.

Armstrong, P. "The *Simpsons* and Democracy: Political Apathy, Popular Culture, and Lifelong Learning as Satire." In R. Hill and R. Kiely (eds.), *Proceedings of the 46th Annual Adult Education Research Conference.* Athens: University of Georgia, 2005b.

Brookfield, S. D. "Media Power and the Development of Media Literacy: An Adult Educational Interpretation." *Harvard Educational Review,* 1986, 56(2), 151–170.

Brown, D. *The Da Vinci Code.* New York: Doubleday, 2003.

Buckingham, D. *Media Education: Literacy, Learning, and Contemporary Culture.* Malden, Mass.: Blackwell, 2003.

Coltrane, S., and Messineo, M. "The Perpetuation of Subtle Prejudice: Race and Gender Imagery in 1990s Television Advertising." *Sex Roles,* 2000, 42(5/6), 363–387.

Considine, D. "Media Literacy: National Developments and International Origins." *Journal of Popular Film and Television,* 2002, 30, 7–15.

Dimitriades, G., and McCarthy, C. "Stranger in the Village: James Baldwin, Popular Culture, and the Ties That Bind." *Qualitative Inquiry,* 2000, 6, 171–187.

Dolby, N. "Popular Culture and Democratic Practice." *Harvard Educational Review,* 2003, 73(3), 258–284.

Eken, A. N. "The Third Eye." *Journal of Adolescent and Adult Literacy,* 2002, 46(3), 220–230.

Freire, P. *Pedagogy of the Oppressed.* New York: Herder & Herder, 1971.

Giroux, H. A. "Cultural Studies, Public Pedagogy, and the Responsibility of Intellectuals." *Communication and Critical/Cultural Studies,* 2004, 1(1), 59–79.

Graham, R. J. "Media Literacy and Cultural Politics." *Adult Education Quarterly,* 1989, 39, 152–160.

Guy, T. C. "Gangsta Rap and Adult Education." In L. Martin and E. Rogers (eds.), *Adult Education in an Urban Context.* New Directions for Adult and Continuing Education, no. 101. San Francisco: Jossey-Bass, 2004.

Hall, A. "Film Reviews and the Public's Perceptions of Stereotypes: Movie Critics' Discourse About *The Siege.*" *Communication Quarterly,* 2001, 49(4), 399–424.

Hamston, J. "Pleasurable Texts: Popular Culture in the Classroom." *Screen Education,* 2002, 37, 107–112.

hooks, b. *Outlaw Culture: Resisting Representation.* New York: Routledge, 1994.

hooks, b. *Reel to Real: Race, Sex, and Class at the Movies.* New York: Routledge, 1996.

Hoppenstand, G. "Country Club Literature and the Thriller." *Journal of Popular Culture,* 2005, *38*(5), 793–795.

Jarvis, C. "Real Stakeholder Education? Lifelong Learning in the Buffyverse." *Studies in the Education of Adults,* 2005, *37*(1), 31–47.

Luke, C. "Media and Cultural Studies in Australia." *Journal of Adolescent and Adult Literacy,* 1999, *42*(8), 622–626.

Miller, N. "Applying Insights from Cultural Studies to Adult Education: What *Seinfeld* Says About the AERC." In A. Rose (ed.), *Proceedings of the 40th Annual Adult Education Research Conference.* DeKalb: Northern Illinois University, 1999.

Noonan, E. "Church Turns 'Da Vinci Code' into Teachable Moment." *Boston Globe,* June 8, 2006.

Pauly, N. "Interpreting Visual Culture as Cultural Narratives in Teacher Education." *Studies in Art Education,* 2003, *44*(3), 264–284.

Quimby, K. "*Will & Grace:* Negotiating (Gay) Marriage on Prime-Time Television." *Journal of Popular Culture,* 2005, *38*(4), 713–730.

Radway, J. *Reading the Romance: Women, Patriarchy, and Popular Literature.* Chapel Hill: University of North Carolina Press, 1984.

Richards, C. "Translations: Encounters with Popular Film and Academic Discourse." *European Journal of Cultural Studies,* 2005, *8*(1), 25–43.

Sandlin, J. A. "Culture, Consumption, and Adult Education: Refashioning Consumer Education for Adults as a Political Site Using a Cultural Studies Framework." *Adult Education Quarterly,* 2005, *55*(3), 165–181.

Tisdell, E. J., and Thompson, P. M. "Seeing 'From a Different Angle': The Role of Pop Culture in Teaching for Diversity and Critical Media Literacy in Adult Education." *International Journal of Lifelong Education,* 26(6), forthcoming.

Yosso, T. "Critical Race Media Literacy: Challenging Deficit Discourses About Chicanos/as." *Journal of Popular Film and Television,* 2002, *30,* 52–62.

ELIZABETH J. TISDELL *is associate professor and coordinator of the Adult Education Doctoral Program at the Pennsylvania State University, Harrisburg.*

2

This chapter focuses on how popular culture can be incorporated into adult classrooms to critically examine the ways in which race, class, and gender identities are constructed in the mass media.

Learning Who We (and They) Are: Popular Culture as Pedagogy

Talmadge C. Guy

In this chapter, I discuss how popular culture has become a major pedagogical project, the path through which most of us learn about ourselves and others. I also suggest some ways that popular culture can be used in educational activities focused on race, class, or gender issues by drawing on examples from my own teaching. In so doing, I want to suggest that although popular culture can be a powerful mechanism for shaping us, it can also be a vehicle for challenging structured inequalities and social injustices. I conclude by arguing that educators of adults can develop powerful educational strategies by employing a critical stance toward popular culture in the activities they design and deliver.

I begin with a reflection on the meaning of education articulated by Benjamin Mays, renowned educator and president of Morehouse College in Atlanta. "Man [sic]," Mays once said, "must live by his dreams, his ideals, the unattainable goal, and what he aspires to be. Man shall not live by bread alone" (1998, p. 488). Mays proposed that the proper source of inspiration for good living (an age-old issue) is one's spiritual life, and education is the process by which people come to this understanding. Attaining self-knowledge and an understanding of one's purpose and place in the world is a vital goal of education, according to Mays. However, in today's global, high-tech world, answers to the critical questions of life are conveyed increasingly through popular culture via the mass media.

NEW DIRECTIONS FOR ADULT AND CONTINUING EDUCATION, no. 115, Fall 2007 © 2007 Wiley Periodicals, Inc.
Published online in Wiley InterScience (www.interscience.wiley.com) • DOI: 10.1002/ace.263

What is popular culture, and why do we enjoy it so much? Popular culture emerged as a concept in nineteenth-century England and was taken to mean the culture of the masses. It was frequently used in contrast to "high culture" (Storey, 1999). Later, popular culture came to be understood as cultural expression that reflected the wisdom of the "folk"—that is, knowledge and values embedded in the lived experiences of people in their strivings for individual and collective fulfillment and meaning. In contrast to these interpretations, critical theorists argue that popular culture serves as a tool that the elite use to dominate the masses (Adorno, 1991; Marcuse, 2002). The important point for the present discussion is that popular culture teaches us about race, class, gender, and other forms of socially significant difference and can reify these differences into social relationships that take on the aura of normalcy.

In this chapter, I understand popular culture "as a site of struggle between the subordinate and the dominant groups in society" (Morrell, 2002, p. 78). Instead of seeing popular culture as simply an imposition of the dominant culture on the marginalized, I prefer the idea of popular culture as a complex interplay of cultural products and meanings placed in circulation by differently positioned persons; these cultural products are simultaneously "received and acted upon" (Dolby, 2003). For example, Elizabeth Tisdell and Patricia Thompson (2006) report on a study of how adult learners construct their own identity based on the award-winning movie *Crash*. This study focused on what adult learners came to understand about the range of cultural identities portrayed in the movie. Nod Miller, Paul Armstrong, and Richard Edwards (2005) explore the ways in which lifestyle-change TV programs promote learning among viewers, who can then also change their identities. One show on the BBC changes women's self-concepts by showing them how to dress. In presenting highly visible, accessible, and appealing examples, pop culture gives adults a vehicle for (re)constructing their identities and for understanding how people who are different have different identities.

Submerged by the Culture Industries

It is tempting to become overly cynical about and critical of pop culture and its influence. Despite the negative aspects of mass-mediated popular culture (pop culture that is manufactured by and disseminated through the major media conglomerates), people are ineluctably drawn to its various forms—whether in music, cinema, TV, radio, or other forms of cultural expression and practice. The reality is that pop culture is popular—in the sense that it is enjoyed by many people. As consumers of pop culture, we want to be entertained, excited, and stimulated. Culture industries such as TV, radio, cinema, the internet, newspapers, magazines, art, and music prolifically develop and disseminate messages about what the society sees as important, valuable, ideal, or desirable. And most Americans are exposed to the

New Directions for Adult and Continuing Education • DOI: 10.1002/ace

products of culture industries much more than to traditional educational content. Consider these facts:

> The average adult watches four to five hours of TV per day.
>
> Four hours of TV programming contain about one hundred ads.
>
> The average American child sees 200,000 violent acts by age eighteen.
>
> The average American youth spends 900 hours in school and 1,023 hours watching TV every year.
>
> Nearly three in four teenagers say that the portrayal of sex on TV influences the sexual behavior of their friends, while one in four says it influences their own.
>
> The average American sees two million commercials by age sixty-five.
>
> Thirty percent of local TV news programming contains ads. [Media Education Foundation, n.d.(a)]

Given the pervasiveness of media-fashioned popular culture, what do the creators of popular culture want? The simple and oft-given answer is—profit. Behind that answer are the mordant effects of advertising and media that exploit consumer desire in order to promote profit (Kilbourne, 1999; Stauber and Rampton, 1995; Williams, 1999). This is a critical point to understand, as Jean Kilbourne (1999, p. 34) aptly observes:

> If you're like most people you think that advertising has no influence on you. This is what advertisers want you to believe. But, if that were true, why would companies spend over $200 billion a year on advertising? Why would they be willing to spend over $250,000 to produce an average television commercial and another $250,000 to air it? If they want to broadcast their commercial during the Super Bowl, they will gladly spend over a million dollars to produce it and over one and a half million to air it. After all, they might have the kind of success that Victoria's Secret did during the 1999 Super Bowl. When they paraded bra-and-panty-clad models across TV screens for a mere thirty seconds, one million people turned away from the game to log on to the Website promoted in the ad. No influence?

Structuring Race, Class, and Gender Through Popular Culture

Brooks and Rada (2002) argue that the media shape our ideas about race through the cultural production of meaning. Critical studies of media and popular culture have produced abundant evidence of just how social structures are reproduced through media. In effect, the mass media produce meanings that form a curriculum through which race, class, and gender are "taught" via cinema, music, TV, radio, advertising, and video (Giroux, 1996; Hall, 1997; hooks, 1996; Kilbourne and others, 2000). Through mass-mediated popular culture we effectively learn what it means to be "white,"

New Directions for Adult and Continuing Education • DOI: 10.1002/ace

"black," "straight," "gay," "middle class," "poor," "wealthy," "Christian," "Muslim," "American," and so on.

For example, images of blacks in the white mind are produced and reinforced by the media through symbolic representations of black "others" that result in the marginalization and demonization of black people as a group. Ron Jacobs's (2000) study of print media shows a clear difference in the way in which blacks are represented in white and black newspapers. Amplifying Jacobs's analysis, Robert Entman and Andrew Rojecki (2000) demonstrate the way in which whites subconsciously develop cognitive "prototypes"—images or caricatures that stand for a whole group—of black people.

Shanie Jamila (2002) argues that race and gender are represented in negative and misogynistic ways in the pop culture of hip hop and rap music (see Chapter Four for an in-depth discussion of this issue). Building on Joan Morgan's work (1999), Jamila points out that black feminism and hip hop have both been an influence on black women. However, the result is a daily living out of the contradictions that exist between these two cultural forms—the honoring and respect for black womanhood versus the pop-culture representation of black women in a misogynistic and negative way. Rather than avoid the contradiction, Jamila believes that black feminists must actively engage with pop culture in order to deconstruct the ways in which it attempts to control the lives of black women. "Teaching women not to be sensual and erotic beings, or not to show that we are, is diminishing and subverts the locus of our own uniqueness as females. Why shouldn't we be able to celebrate our beauty, sensuality, sexuality, creative ability or our eroticism? They are all unique sites of women's power that we should not be taught to hide, or only display when someone else says it's appropriate" (Jamila, 2002, p. 393).

Jean Kilbourne's (1999) research on the representation of women in advertising provides strong evidence of the ways in which popular culture can influence societal views of women's body image and of gender roles. She argues that the objectification of women is popularized through a system of advertising production and dissemination. Female body parts become mere "tools for the advertising trade" (Van Eman, 2005, p. 90). In the end, the messages teach that the product is more important than the person.

White female beauty, in particular, as a cultural standard is enacted through the media, as is evidenced by the popular fascination with attractive women from celebrities like Paris Hilton and the late Anna Nicole Smith to star athletes like Anna Kournikova and Maria Sharapova. Notions of physical beauty and desirability become visibly reinforced in the minds of adults and children. The objectification of women combined with conspicuous consumption instills the idea that anyone should be able to have anything that makes one feel good.

The pervasive subtlety by which this process occurs can be alarming. For example, as I was riding on I-285 in Atlanta to a relative's house,

I observed a sign advertising home generators that can be used when residential electric power is interrupted. The sign has a picture of a young, buxom, blond woman clad in a tight, red, sleeveless dress with the caption "We promise to get you into hot water!" The double-entendre message is immediately comprehensible to a homeowner, male or female.

Beyond the obvious point—that "sex sells"—was it only coincidence that the woman was white, blond, buxom, and was wearing a tight, red dress? Each of these markers signals a particular set of cultural attributes that, taken together, not only represent a highly desirable form of female beauty but are expressions of a dominant ideology that is both racist and patriarchal; it is indeed no accident that blond, white, thin, buxom women are frequently seen in commercials advertising everything from whisky to home generators.

Commercials have become more about selling sex than about products; reducing female and male models to sexual adjectives often involves making sexually stimulating commercials in which a product is displayed. When viewing media with my students and family, I have begun asking, "What is this commercial selling?" Very often the answer is "sex" or "companionship." If we begin to view others as objects, we no longer feel any responsibility toward them as people but instead view them as things. We no longer think of them as having feelings, ideas, souls, or even value. For us as consumers, people then become solely a commodity—something else to be owned, acquired, bought, or sold. Sex is removed from interpersonal intimacy and becomes a trite tool of advertising, to be displayed on billboards constantly viewed by the public. No longer is monogamy thought of as the norm for citizens. The media messages teach that sex is everywhere and should be sought in all circumstances and places with anyone we desire. As educators of adults, then, we need a way to help ourselves and our learners critically examine these corrosive and dehumanizing messages of popular culture.

Critically Analyzing Pop Culture: Some Examples from Practice

Henry Giroux (1996) sees popular culture as a domain where democracy and social-justice ideals can be given priority through critical educational processes. I have endeavored to incorporate examples of popular culture into classroom activities and assignments to help adults interrogate the ways in which race, class, and gender are represented through media. I have discovered that classroom energy levels rise substantially as students engage with the examples and discuss various perspectives regarding popular culture and its implications.

For example, I teach a multicultural-issues class where race, class, and gender are organizing themes for examining structured inequalities. In one assignment I ask students to engage in critical analysis of media by selecting a TV series to watch and then reporting on the ways in which race, class, and gender are represented. The assignment calls for students to consider how different people (men, women, white, black, Hispanic) are portrayed. I adapt a critical-viewing learning tool from the Media Education Foundation (n.d.(a)) to ask: What is the appearance of the people in the program? What colors are used to frame the scenes? What camera angles are used? What sounds or background music are employed? What feelings are evoked by the way in which the scenes or episodes are presented? Are different ethnicities, genders, and races consistently portrayed in particular ways? What ads support the program? To whom do the ads appeal? How do the ads portray race, class, or gender issues?

One student reported on the TV series *Commander in Chief,* starring Geena Davis as Mackenzie Allen, president of the United States. During the discussion of the episode, we examined the way in which gender was represented in the person of a woman president who possessed feminine qualities such as attractiveness, sincerity, and compassion. The student reported that despite being witty, intelligent, and ethical, President Allen often displayed weakness and deference to men. In one scene, she attempted to appease her jealous husband. The episode provided much content with which to examine gender and power and to unpack the issues that confront women in leadership roles.

In another assignment, I ask students to review excerpts from the award-winning movie *Crash.* Students are asked to identify and discuss the cultural dynamics in play during each of the scenes. In one especially difficult and poignant scene an affluent, light-skinned African American couple are stopped at a red light while driving home in their luxury SUV from a gala. Suspicious of what appears to be a sexual interlude between the couple, two white male police officers discuss what is going on in the couple's car. What begins as a routine traffic stop quickly devolves into an ugly scene in which the wife is physically body searched by one of the officers while the husband, standing spread-eagled against his car, is forced to watch. The scene concludes with the husband offering an apology for whatever inappropriate behavior the police have perceived and pleads to be released with his wife.

As students discuss the scene, they identify several racial, gender, class, and power dynamics at work. Frequently, students express their disgust with the scene but often acknowledge, some for the first time, the way in which African Americans may have justifiable fear of and disdain for police power. They also consider the extent to which the African American husband is or is not justified in acquiescing to police while witnessing his wife being sexually manhandled by one of them. Furthermore, they consider the way in which skin tone can play a part in the racial stereotyping of black–white romantic relationships because the African American wife is so fair-skinned that she could be mistaken for white.

In considering classroom activities and assignments such as these, I have found it important to avoid imposing my analysis on students. Sometimes

New Directions for Adult and Continuing Education • DOI: 10.1002/ace

students have different interpretations of the pop-culture examples that I use. Although I offer my own analysis, I find that it is pedagogically effective to simply have students consider the multiple ways in which race, class, gender issues can be read. I also ask learners to consider the intent of the producers and to contrast this analysis with their own or other students' interpretations. Because many students have tacitly acknowledged the ways in which media and pop culture frame race, class, and gender, sometimes they point out how enlightening and energizing it is to critically analyze the way in which race, class, or gender hierarchies are represented and reproduced. In these kinds of discussions the development of a critical media literacy enables students to reconsider and critique pop culture and media rather than taking them for granted.

Learners need a framework for critiquing popular culture. Luke (1999) identifies four forms of critical media literacy for analyzing texts: coding practice, text-meaning practice, pragmatic practice, and critical practice. Coding practice involves a set of skills useful in cracking the code of a particular text. The key question to ask is "How does the text work?" (p. 623). In the highway-billboard advertisement of home electric generators, how do the woman's youth, blondness, whiteness, buxomness, and sexy, red dress encode messages about the desirability of electric generators? What do these codes have to do with homeowners who, in bad weather, want to restore power to their homes? What does the phrase "hot water" encode? By considering the codes that are used to convey meaning, we can begin to unpack the not-so-subtle messages about sex and electricity implicit in this advertisement.

Text-meaning practices are ways in which the text embeds particular ideological frames of reference. The pedagogical goal is to uncover the hidden, ideological aspects of the text. In the analysis of *Commander in Chief,* the critical-viewing task involves uncovering the unstated but evident ways in which women as leaders are portrayed. Analyzing how Geena Davis is asked to play the role of president and how she interacts with the other actors in the series produces a text for understanding messages about women in powerful roles.

Pragmatic practice consists of determining the different interpretations that can be made by different identity groups in different contexts. In the police scene from *Crash,* how do white women and African American women see the issues of gender and race? How do African American men and African American women read the dynamics of male interaction when safety and security are at stake? What do these different "readings" have to say about our own positionality (for example, our gender, race, class, or sexual orientation) and the way in which we construct race, class, and gender identities?

Finally, critical practice refers to the way in which we challenge popular-culture representations. Mass-mediated popular culture is marketed to particular demographic groups. The question to be asked is what groups are being marketed to and what meanings and representations are being marketed to them? How are particular messages of mass-mediated pop culture received by different sociocultural groups? What are the ways in which these patterns of meanings can be challenged? What are the implications for changing our individual behaviors toward these messages? What are some ways in which we can organize to combat the coercive effects of such messages?

Conclusion

How should educators of adults understand the critique of pop culture in their work? Popular culture is a contested domain of social life in which multiple interpretations of meaning are taken by both producers and consumers and by educators of adults and adult learners. Educators of adults can employ the activities and strategies suggested here to help learners engage constructively with race, class, and gender issues. In this area of multiplicity and complexity lies the potential for developing a critical analysis and awareness of the ways in which pop culture constrains, controls, and circumscribes attitudes and behaviors as well as liberates, creates, and expands awareness.

In the last analysis, the goal should be to help adults learn to establish creative and wholesome relationships with others, to live in harmony and cooperation, and to find meaning in life beyond the mundane, the material, and the superficial. The goal of education, as Mays says, is to live by our "dreams, . . . ideals, the unattainable goal, and what [we aspire] to be."

References

Adorno, T. W. *The Culture Industry: Selected Essays on Mass Culture.* (J. M. Bernstein, trans.). London: Routledge, 1991.

Brooks, D. E., and Rada, J. A. "Constructing Race in Black and Whiteness: Media Coverage of Public Support for President Clinton." *Journalism & Communication Monographs,* 2002, *113*(44), 115–156.

Dolby, N. "Popular Culture and Democratic Practice." *Harvard Educational Review,* 2003, *73*(3), 258–284.

Entman, R. M., and Rojecki, A. *The Black Image in the White Mind: Media and Race in America.* Chicago: University of Chicago Press, 2000.

Giroux, H. A. "Democratic Education and Popular Culture." *International Journal of Social Work,* 1996, *11*(1), 59–69.

Hall, S. (ed.). *Representation: Cultural Representations and Signifying Practices.* In Culture, Media, and Identities series. Thousand Oaks, Calif.: Sage, 1997.

hooks, b. *Reel to Real: Race, Sex, and Class at the Movies.* New York: Routledge, 1996.

Jacobs, R. N. *Race, Media, and the Crisis of Civil Society: From Watts to Rodney King.* Cambridge, U.K.: Cambridge University Press, 2000.

Jamila, S. "Can I Get a Witness? Testimony from a Hip-Hop Feminist." In D. Hernandez and B. Rehman (eds.), *Colonize This: Women of Color on Today's Feminism.* New York: Seal Press, 2002.

Kilbourne, J. *Deadly Persuasion: Why Women and Girls Must Fight the Addictive Power of Advertising.* New York: Free Press, 1999.

Kilbourne, J., and others. *Killing Us Softly 3: Advertising's Image of Women.* Northampton, Mass.: Media Education Foundation, 2000. Videotape.

Luke, C. "Media and Cultural Studies in Australia." *Journal of Adolescent and Adult Literacy,* 1999, 42(8), 622–626.

Marcuse, H. *One-Dimensional Man: Studies in the Ideology of Advanced Industrial Society.* New York: Routledge, 2002.

Mays, B. E. "What Man Lives By." In S. Barboza (ed.), *African American Book of Values: Classic Moral Stories.* New York: Bantam Books, 1998.

Media Education Foundation, "Deconstructing a Video Advertisement," n.d.(a). Retrieved July 10, 2005, from http://www.mediaed.org/handouts/pdfs/Deconstruct VideoAd.pdf.

Media Education Foundation, "Ten Reasons Why Media Education Matters," n.d.(b). Retrieved July 10, 2005, from http://www.mediaed.org/handouts/pdfs/10Reasons Poster.pdf.

Miller, N., Armstrong, P., and Edwards, R. "Learning to Be Different: Identity, Embodiment and Popular Culture." In P. Armstrong (ed.), *Standing Conference on University Teaching and Research in the Education of Adults.* Sussex, U.K.: University of Sussex, 2005.

Morell, E. "Toward a Critical Pedagogy of Popular Culture: Literacy Development Among Urban Youth." *Journal of Adolescent and Adult Literacy,* 2002, 46(1), 72–77.

Morgan, J. *When Chickenheads Come Home to Roost: My Life as a Hip-Hop Feminist.* New York: Simon & Schuster, 1999.

Stauber, J. C., and Rampton, S. *Toxic Sludge Is Good for You: Lies, Damn Lies and the Public Relations Industry.* Monroe, Maine: Common Courage Press, 1995.

Storey, J. *Cultural Consumption and Everyday Life: Cultural Studies in Practice.* New York: Oxford University Press, 1999.

Tisdell, E. J., and Thompson, P. M. "*Crash*-ing into Pop Culture in Dealing with Diversity: Adult Education and Critical Media Literacy About Movies and Television." In *Proceedings of the 47th Annual Adult Education Research Conference.* Minneapolis: University of Minnesota, 2006.

Van Eman, S. *On Earth as It Is in Advertising: Moving from Commercial Hype to Gospel Hope.* Grand Rapids, Mich.: Brazos Press, 2005.

Williams, R. "Advertising: The Magic System." In S. During (ed.), *The Cultural Studies Reader.* London: Routledge, 1999.

TALMADGE C. GUY is associate professor of adult education in the Department of Lifelong Education, Administration, and Policy at the University of Georgia.

3

This chapter describes the use of popular film and semiotics for the development of critical media literacy in a graduate-level education course.

Critical Media Literacy and Popular Film: Experiences of Teaching and Learning in a Graduate Class

Heather Stuckey, Kelly Kring

We make meaning in powerful ways through many types of media, with movies being one of the particularly relevant forms. Movie viewers often discuss characters with whom they relate, and their comments often reflect parts of their own narratives. Because of this strong identification with the characters, many authors have considered the use of film in different contexts (Buckingham, 2003; Grace, 2005; Hesley and Hesley, 2001). Movies can also be a particularly useful tool for developing critical media literacy in educational settings; they help students learn how to analyze the ways in which gender, race, ethnicity, class, and sexual orientation (referred to collectively in the remainder of this chapter as *social relations*) are portrayed in a film.

In this chapter we discuss our experiences analyzing how social relations are portrayed in popular film in a graduate course entitled Pop Culture as Pedagogy: The Role of Entertainment Media in Teaching for Critical Consciousness and Critical Media Literacy. One of us (Heather Stuckey) team-taught the course with two colleagues (the editors of this volume), and the other of us (Kelly Kring) was a student in the course. The course focused on analysis of different forms of pop culture, specifically on film and television, as a way of revealing how social relations are based on structural issues of power. All the students in the course were graduate students

and were either K–12 teachers or adult educators. We focus here on how film was used in the course to develop critical media literacy.

Among the course requirements, several related to the use of film: students were to analyze their favorite movie as an opening assignment; watch specific movies because of their portrayals of race, gender, sexual orientation, and class; and to develop an educational activity intended to develop critical media literacy in their own educational practices. All films were chosen by either the instructors or the class; they included *Crash* (2005), *Far from Heaven* (2002), *Whale Rider* (2002), and *The Hours* (2002). Most students also elected to see *Brokeback Mountain* (2005) because of its direct portrayal of sexual orientation, and the movie became the subject of much discussion both inside the classroom and out.

Both of us are moviegoers and avid consumers of popular culture, and we wanted to participate in the course because of our passion for it. We worked on this chapter together because of our fascination with film and our interest in creativity and imagination in learning. Our goal was to discover the ways in which media use images and symbols to communicate messages about cultural themes. The chapter is divided into three sections: our own initial journeys from experience to analysis; the ways we constructed knowledge through class and online; and how to incorporate popular culture and media into practice.

Beginning the Journey, From Experience to Analysis

Both of us are white, middle-class women. We grew up watching shows like *Charlie's Angels* and *The Captain and Tennille,* thinking very little about how women were portrayed in these television shows and even less about the lack of racial diversity in the main characters. As we entered into philosophical discussions of feminist theories throughout our doctoral program, we began to interpret the effects of oppression (as female) and privilege (as white) on our cultural identities. In this section, we discuss how media intersect with our construction of identity through our backgrounds and then through our experiences taking and teaching this course.

Heather's Story. Growing up in South Central Pennsylvania in a small German family where I was the only child, I had to meet certain expectations. I could not talk back to my father, I had to respect those in authority, and I had to keep quiet unless asked to speak, especially because I was a girl. Although in public I tried to pretend I didn't notice, I felt the oppression as deeply as the snow fell in Oswego this year (nearly twelve feet, as I understand). So, when I went to the movies for the first time to see *Pete's Dragon* (1977), I unsurprisingly noticed that a boy, Pete, not a girl, was the main character. Even the dragon, Elliott, was male. Since then, I have seen countless movies and television shows, and the theme of gender and cultural positioning still remains an issue in them.

New Directions for Adult and Continuing Education • DOI: 10.1002/ace

I wanted to teach this course because of my interest in the use of symbols to portray thematic elements of movies and in the ways in which semiotics plays a role in the reinforcement of or the resistance to cultural stereotypes. In brief, semiotics is an analysis of symbols or anything that signifies something within a culture. According to Ferdinand de Sausserre (Berger, 2005), a *sign* has two elements, that of *the signifier* and that of *the signified*, with the signifier representing the form and the signified representing the associated conceptual understanding provoked by viewing an image—in other words, its meaning. In a similar way, Barthes (1964) refers to the denotation of an image, or a literal meaning, and the connotation, the meaning of a sign that is given through the cultural experiences a reader brings to it. For meaning to be constructed, these two elements must exist *in relation* and be interpreted by the viewer of the image. Although the images (signifier or denotation) remain relatively stable, the interpretations and meanings of those images (signified or connotation) shift over time. Raising awareness of the symbolic nature of media can help to challenge the assumptions of what is considered "normal" in the dominant culture and bring about increased sensitivity to issues of inclusion.

From a semiotic perspective, the analysis of signs and symbols can uncover hidden assumptions about race, gender, and other cultural differences. An initial strategy I wanted to try in the classroom was to use static images—photos or particular scenes—of different racial groups and sexual orientations to illustrate the messages the symbols were communicating. The meanings given to the images are often in the form of codes, which are "organized around key oppositions and equations in which a term like 'woman' is defined in opposition to a term like 'man,' and in which each term is aligned with a cluster of symbolic attributes" (Silverman, 1983, p. 36). By bringing encoded messages in images to an open awareness, we were making the unconscious explicit, while acknowledging the possibility of multiple interpretations. Semiotics teaches us how to decipher these messages and "bring them to consciousness" (Berger, 2005, p. 15). After students reflected on these cultural messages in static photos, then we could incorporate that knowledge into films and television shows in order to analyze the settings, time period, the directors' perspective, and aspects of cultural identities.

Kelly's Story. I am a doctoral student in adult education and decided to take the course because I'm an avid fan of pop culture and I realize the influence pop culture has on my worldview. I enjoy movies and reality shows, and I realize how certain shows, such as *Seinfeld* and its catch phrases, influence our culture. As an instructor of adults, teaching in the field of early-childhood education, I use media in the classroom to support content and to reach students using different strategies from the typical ones often found in classroom settings. I took the class in critical media literacy to learn how media could be used in the classroom to support learning and to promote critical thinking.

New Directions for Adult and Continuing Education • DOI: 10.1002/ace

I also thought the class would challenge me to view media from a different perspective because I typically watch shows or films from an entertainment viewpoint. Watching films is a pleasurable activity for me, and I view this medium from a primarily egocentric viewpoint, typically asking, "How does this show affect me personally and how does it entertain me?" Until I took this class, I rarely questioned motivations or other agendas that may have influenced what I was watching. This course encouraged me to look beyond the surface to examine the social, political, or financial motives that influence what is shared on the screen.

In this course, as an opening assignment, we were asked to critically analyze our favorite movie (mine was *The Way We Were*, 1973), and we were given a set of questions to guide our analysis. I had always watched the movie for the romantic aspect, but I decided to research the political perspective of the movie and discovered information about the Hollywood Ten and the blacklisting that occurred during the time period in which the film was set. I didn't know anything about that topic before I wrote the paper and investigated below the surface of the movie. When the film was released, the director cut many of the political statements because the audience wanted the film to focus on the love story, not the political quagmire, and the studio wanted the film to make money and fit into the mainstream. Barbra Streisand, one of the stars, was not pleased with the edits and fought strongly to keep the political scenes in the movie, but ultimately the studio had the financial power to determine the final version (*The Way We Were*, 1999). Analyzing all these events helped me develop my own critical media awareness and literacy.

Constructing Knowledge: Together in Class or Online

Because watching movies is generally a source of pleasure, it is easy to get learners engaged in doing so, but, based on the opening assignments, that sense of pleasure can sometimes get in the way of students' ability to look at their favorite movie critically (Hamston, 2002). Ali Nihat Eken (2002) suggests drawing on this sense of pleasure. However, he recommends the use of the "third eye" (the ability to look beyond the content of the film and view it from a critical perspective) to improve students' media literacy, and to raise "awareness of the power of the human mind to interpret clues . . . ; through this awareness, students learn to think critically and analytically and engage in creative expression" (p. 228). By looking at the cinematic aspects of the film (such as lighting or camera angles), the dramatic aspects (the acting and costumes), and the literary aspects (narrative, setting, and symbols), students can analyze how these aspects of the movie resist or reinforce the dominant culture. One way we began our class discussions was to focus on the narrative and the way the story line either implicitly or explicitly reinforced dominant-culture notions of social relations and structural binaries such as black/white, male/female, hetero-sexual/homosexual.

Many films rely on structural binaries to reproduce or challenge access to power in the dominant culture (Jones, 2006; Silverman, 1983). When the binaries are challenged, such as homosexuality and heterosexuality in *Brokeback Mountain* and *Far from Heaven*, male and female roles in *Whale Rider* and *The Hours*, or white and racial "other" in *Crash*, the film can open up discussion about cultural issues and social relations. Most of the class chose to watch *Brokeback Mountain*, and much of the discussion of the film was held online. In our discussion, we determined how the movie both rein-forced and challenged the binaries of sexual orientation in the dominant culture. We use this discussion as an example here to explain how assump-tions were uncovered and new knowledge constructed in the development of critical media literacy. Similar discussions took place about the other films used in the class.

Brokeback Mountain is a drama based on the short story by Annie Proulx, published by the *New Yorker* in 1997. The story explores the lives of two white cowboys who meet during the summer of 1963 while herding sheep on Brokeback Mountain. They fall in love and have a sexual relationship, yet cave to the pressure of compulsory heterosexuality. Both men marry women, although they continue their relationship with each other. One of the men, Jack, is killed, and it is left for the viewer to decide whether he was mur-dered because of his homosexuality or whether he was killed in an accident while changing a tire, which is the story his wife tells. Ennis, his lover, finds out about Jack's death after receiving a returned postcard marked "deceased," and Ennis moves to Brokeback Mountain, where he can remember Jack.

After discussing online and in class the many underlying themes of the movie, such as the setting, the complex relationship that developed between the main characters, and the use of camera angles, many participants began to increase their level of analysis, both about how characters were portrayed and also about the use of symbols from a semiotics perspective. When watching a film, viewers can have one interpretation of a symbol, but when they begin to construct knowledge with others, many other possible meanings and interpretations can come to light (Gergen, 1999). One exam-ple of the social construction of knowledge was in our dialogue about a scene in which Jack sees Ennis's reflection in a rearview mirror and about the metaphor of the rearview mirror itself. One participant noted it sym-bolized the pain of letting go of something one deeply wants yet is unable to have. Another suggested it represented the fact that Ennis and Jack's rela-tionship could not be held in public view. These types of dialogue about the possible meanings of a film help us construct knowledge collectively and add layers of analysis and meaning to the text.

It was our assumption that all films are constructions that were made by someone in a position of power (the director, the producers, the film company), and they all reflect a point of view. As such, the powerful images in *Brokeback* were not just accidental placements but were conveying a message. The multiple possible interpretations of any image vary not only by individual perceptions of the moment but also by the positionality of the viewers (their gender, race, class, sexual orientation) and their life experiences. For example, in one scene the sheep owner who employs Jack and Ennis is watching through his binoculars as Jack and Ennis roll in the fields on Brokeback Mountain. Later, the owner denies Jack some of his pay and does not allow Jack and Ennis to work the fields at the end of the season. During an online discussion, one openly gay male student in reflecting on the scene noted that the "virulent homophobia [of the sheep owner] smacked me in the face." The students went on to note the many who have been looked at "through binoculars" and judged by others. As a class, we reflected on how media culture often encodes a system of ideas that legitimizes heterosexuality. We generally agreed *Brokeback* challenged the dominant culture because homosexual or bisexual relationships are not often portrayed in serious ways. In the classroom, opening up a dialogue about movie characters (as opposed to people in the class) is a way for students to feel comfortable talking about controversial issues.

We all bring our own understandings to a classroom discussion based on our experience and philosophical perspective. Discussion is part of the learning because the social interaction helps both the teacher and the learner see multiple interpretations and to raise awareness to a conscious level. Our understanding of how homophobia affects the lives of those who are straight and those who are sexual minorities expanded significantly the more we reflected internally and discussed outwardly with others to reconstruct meaning. Many in the class, particularly the women, thought that Jack and Ennis's first sexual encounter seemed aggressive and somewhat violent. Through dialogue, we reflected on their aggressiveness as a symbol of a lack of intimacy and of their fight against entering into a homosexual relationship with each other. This conversation about a movie dealing with current controversial issues helped raise awareness and consciousness of the privileges that heterosexuals have in society. This increase in awareness was facilitated partially by the fact that there was an openly gay man in the class, as well as others who spoke openly about how their sexual orientation and other aspects of their positionality, particularly gender, seemed to be at play in their analysis of the movie.

It isn't always easy to teach critical media literacy by bringing the invisible out into the open or unveiling our unconscious assumptions. Images and messages that surround us both resist and reinforce the dominant culture, but we often fail to recognize them. It is like trying to remember the images on a dime. Coins become so much a part of our lives that we don't take the time to examine them. As critical media-literacy educators, we are bringing the unseen into sight and the invisible into the visible realm.

New Directions for Adult and Continuing Education • DOI: 10.1002/ace

The development of critical media literacy doesn't happen overnight. The point of critical media literacy is not necessarily to change people's political viewpoints or their perspectives on issues; rather, it is to help them bring portrayals in the media to consciousness. For example, clearly some people in the class disapproved of gay relationships. But, by looking at the movie critically, they recognized that the film was about many relationships, not only that of Ennis and Jack but also those of the men and their families. There were nearly as many heterosexual kisses in the movie as homosexual. Although the dominant culture might say the movie was about gay men because that part is "different" from the dominant culture, the similarity is the struggle we all face when we choose to be in a relationship with another, regardless of the gender. As one student pondered toward the end of class, "I wonder if sexuality and sexual desire aren't more on a continuum. . . . Some people clearly exist at one end or the other . . . but others exist somewhere in between." These types of realizations challenge the binaries, in this case of gay/straight, and begin discussions on which all of us can reflect.

Taking It to Practice

One of the other assignments in this course was to develop and implement a practical project on media and learning that included an introduction of an issue, an explanation of the theoretical grounding, an outline of the project, and a summary piece commenting on what the students learned from the project. As an instructor of directors in the child-care and early-education field, Kelly chose the film *Daddy Day Care* (2003) for students to critically analyze. The movie depicts two fathers who open up a child-care center, yet have little experience with children. The purpose of analyzing the movie was to think about the role media has played in depicting the profession of child care, how the portrayal affected the students' conception of the field, and how it influences society's interpretation of the profession. In analyzing the film from a critical view, we also examined how race, gender, and class were represented.

Some of the child-care directors questioned whether the film made child-care employees look inferior or incompetent because the two fathers in the movie say, "How hard can it be? It's just babysitting." The child-care industry has been fighting this viewpoint because many people in the field get advanced teaching or professional degrees. Some of the child-care directors realized that society will watch films like this one and not question the negative message it is sending about child care. All the students in the class were white and women. Many of them said, "That's child care. That's the field." In general, this is the response of many Americans who watch movies for entertainment and pleasure, but "if Americans reject critical analysis of popular culture and other media texts, they reject analysis of a significant portion of their life activity" (Rockler, 2002, p. 17).

In teaching critical media literacy, it is important to point out the positionality of characters. In *Daddy Day Care,* for example, it is men—fathers—who are featured. In a way, the juxtaposition of cultural norms makes the film comical, but students of critical media literacy also have to think about how the movie reinforces the dominant culture's view that babysitting is women's work. Both of us use movies in the classroom to talk about these issues from a "safe" distance and to engage the students in learning. A more traditional way of teaching is to say to the students, "Let's talk about the child-care industry," and then use facts and figures; but numbers aren't enough. Using movies is an alternative way of exploring a potentially controversial topic without using numerical facts, but with multiple interpretations of a film's cinematic, dramatic, and literary symbolisms.

Conclusion

We learned about critical media literacy not only from our experience in the class but also from writing this chapter. As one of the instructors, Heather learned not to assume that students know what is meant by looking at a subject critically. Showing images of examples, particularly images of dominant-culture themes, helps students understand and process the first layer of looking at a subject with a critical eye. For instance, in *Brokeback Mountain* students quickly picked up on the theme of homosexuality and how it was portrayed on various levels throughout the movie, but they didn't comment as much on the heterosexual marriages of Ennis and Jack. Pointing out the hidden messages of sexuality, because they are common in the dominant culture, was necessary to help students become aware of their own positionality.

As a student in the class, Kelly learned the importance of examining below the surface of entertainment media and all media to discover other agendas, influences, and positions that affect the final film, television show, or news broadcast. All education, all media portrayal, is political, and as we have discovered in our studies in adult education, to examine critically is to gain a deeper knowledge of the process and the content of the material (Browne, 2005). The research Kelly reviewed that related to the making of *The Way We Were* led to a much more meaningful understanding of the political and social influences that affected the final product than we would have otherwise had.

As teachers of critical media literacy, we are constantly challenged to use media in new, instructive ways based on the interests of the students and the political direction of our culture. As students, we also become teachers, constructing new knowledge collectively and bringing our own experience to the classroom. Using popular film is one way to make that happen.

References

Barthes, R. *Elements of Semiology.* (Annette Lavers and Colin Smith, trans.). New York: Hill & Wang, 1964.

Berger, A. *Making Sense of Media.* Oxford: Blackwell, 2005.

Brokeback Mountain. Directed by Ang Lee and written by Annie Proulx. Paramount Pictures, 2005.

Browne, R. *Popular Culture Studies Across the Curriculum.* Jefferson, N.C.: McFarland, 2005.

Buckingham, D. *Media Education: Literacy, Learning, and Contemporary Culture.* Malden, Mass.: Blackwell, 2003.

Crash. Directed and written by Paul Haggis. Lionsgate Studios, 2005.

Daddy Day Care. Directed by Steve Carr and written by Geoff Rodkey. Revolution Studios, 2003.

Eken, A. N. "The Third Eye." *Journal of Adolescent and Adult Literacy,* 2002, 46(3), 220–230.

Far from Heaven. Directed and written by Todd Haynes. Clear Blue Sky Productions, 2002.

Gergen, K. J. *An Invitation to Social Construction.* Thousand Oaks, Calif.: Sage, 1999.

Grace, M. *Reel Fulfillment.* New York: McGraw-Hill, 2005.

Hamston, J. "Pleasurable Texts: Popular Culture in the Classroom." *Screen Education,* 2002, 37, 107–112.

Hesley, J. W., and Hesley, J. G. *Rent Two Films and Let's Talk in the Morning: Using Popular Movies in Psychotherapy.* (2nd ed.). New York: Wiley, 2001.

The Hours. Directed by Stephen Daldry and written by Michael Cunningham. Paramount Pictures, 2002.

Jones, J. "It's a Fine Line Between Pleasure and Pain: Representations of Masculinity in 'Gladiator.'" *Screen Education,* 2006, 43, 110–115.

Pete's Dragon. Directed by Don Chaffey and written by S. S. Field. Walt Disney Productions, 1977.

Rockler, N. R. "Overcoming 'It's Just Entertainment': Perspective by Incongruity as Strategy for Media Literacy." *Journal of Popular Film and Television,* 2002, 30(1), 16–22.

Silverman, K. *The Subject of Semiotics.* New York: Oxford University Press, 1983.

The Way We Were. Directed by Sydney Pollack and written by Arthur Laurents. Columbia Pictures, 1973.

The Way We Were Twenty-Fifth Anniversary Special Edition. "Making of" Documentary: *Looking Back.* Directed by Sydney Pollack and written by Arthur Larents. Columbia Pictures, 1999.

Whale Rider. Directed by Niki Caro and written by Witi Ihimaera. New Zealand Film Corp., 2002.

HEATHER STUCKEY has a doctorate in adult education from the Pennsylvania State University, Harrisburg, and works there in the Office of Research and Graduate Studies.

KELLY KRING is a doctoral student in adult education at the Pennsylvania State University, Harrisburg.

This chapter discusses how to draw on hip hop as a culturally relevant tool for teaching educators and adult learners to read the word, the world, and the media.

Old School Crossings: Hip Hop in Teacher Education and Beyond

Mary Stone Hanley

Every generation has a musical score that marks its passing through the world, and people of previous generations often resist displacement of their music. However, "old school" educators who understand the importance of popular music in the lives of most adolescents and young adults have a rich pool of learning possibilities from which to draw. Inquiry into and engagement with the popular culture of rising generations can inform curricular choices of educators, both those working with adults in teacher-education programs and those working with children. I try to highlight these connections in my work with both preservice teachers and graduate students as I teach critical multicultural education and arts education.

Ernest Morrell (2002) defines popular culture as the terrain of ideological struggle expressed through music, film, mass media, artifacts, language, customs, and values. Robert Price (2005) views hip hop culture as an ideological paradigm shift that challenges the worldviews of former generations. Ideologies emerge from historical contexts, and hip hop is an expression of the contradictions youth experienced at the end of the twentieth century and continue to experience in the new millennium (George, 1998; Guy, 2004; Ogg and Upshal, 2001; Rose, 1994). Price suggests that members of older generations who criticize hip hop without investigation are wallowing in stereotypes and bias. He further asserts that as long as there is a gap between providers of adult education and their students, "the need of adult learners will not be met" (p. 55). Talmadge Guy (2004), in introducing hip hop to the field of adult education, discussed some implications

NEW DIRECTIONS FOR ADULT AND CONTINUING EDUCATION, no. 115, Fall 2007 © 2007 Wiley Periodicals, Inc.
Published online in Wiley InterScience (www.interscience.wiley.com) • DOI: 10.1002/ace.265

for adult education in general. Here, I discuss the use of hip hop with a specific group of adult learners: the educators I serve in teacher-education programs and, ultimately, their students as well. I draw on hip hop as a way to model using dialogic instruction, the arts, and popular culture to develop literacy skills in the broad sense—to teach how to read the word, the world, and the media—as well as how to draw on people's creative agency.

Critical multicultural education requires that students develop a critical consciousness to interrogate the dominant paradigm; imagination and creativity are essential for visualizing a world of possibilities in the classroom and beyond. Through research on hip hop I model the sort of inquiry I expect of my students: I want them to be able to examine the complexities and dynamics of a culture and to question hegemonic representations. In this way I stay in touch with the cultural understandings of undergraduate and graduate students who consider themselves a part of the hip hop generation; I am thus a more informed and approachable educator than I would otherwise be, and having these characteristics is important for transformative teaching. In this chapter I explain how hip hop informs my pedagogy with adult students by first sharing some of my own journey as I learned about hip hop and then explaining how I use it in my educational practice.

Learning About Hip Hop: Educating the Educator

For me, as an African American youth growing up in the middle twentieth century in the black community of an industrial city in the northeastern United States, music, especially rhythm and blues, was the salient form of mass popular culture. The tales told and questions raised in songs informed my relationships and narratives. Singers like Aretha Franklin, Marvin Gaye, and Jerry Butler provided me with visions of power and love, a moral compass, and a perspective on black culture that was lyrical, rhythmical, emotional, dynamic, communal, resistant, and pleasurable. They provided a standard of excellence during a time when little of black excellence was represented in the mass media. For me and my peers black popular music represented an alternative space we proudly claimed in opposition to white claims of superiority.

That experience informed my thinking when I began to study the music and culture of hip hop while working with a thirteen-year-old African American student in a drama program. She had been suspended from school so many times that her graduation from middle school was in jeopardy. This same youngster passionately read and authoritatively discussed the lives and works of emcees and disc jockeys (djs) and other aspects of hip hop culture. The contradiction between her obvious intelligence and her school performance led me to wonder how hip hop, this distortion of what I understood to be music, could hook this youngster and engage her in such ardent learning.

New Directions for Adult and Continuing Education • DOI: 10.1002/ace

To learn more I listened to the music and read lyrics on Ohhla.com, a hip hop lyrics Web site. I also had informal conversations with teenagers, ages sixteen to nineteen, and young adults, ages twenty to twenty-six, and I interviewed six emcees, ages twenty-two to thirty-six, about their involvement in hip hop, the issues of violence and misogyny, and the role of hip hop in the social structure. I went to several dance clubs and open mics where emcees and djs presented their words, rhythms, and music. I began with the study of the history of commercial hip hop and quickly found myself investigating an "underground" culture of artistic agency, African diasporic culture and aesthetics, literacy, music, economics, and pleasure constructed by late adolescents and young adults as an expression of their experience. I found that hip hop is a broad culture with many forms of meaning-making including graffiti art, dance, and dejaying. Rap music is only one aspect of hip hop culture, and it has multiple perspectives and meanings.

In order to understand the educational possibilities in the words and performance of hip hop music and poetry, it is important to understand the history of hip hop and the economic conditions that spawned it. Hip hop began in the mid-1970s in the South Bronx of New York City, a wasteland of demolished and abandoned buildings, poverty, and a limited economic base. From these bleak conditions emerged an expressive culture of resistance in which youth groups made music, danced, and created graffiti art about their rage, alienation, resistance, and desires. The economic background of hip hop enables a discussion of capitalist wealth and poverty and the role of the arts in exposing those contradictions.

Rap began at community dances when djs played a back track of musical beats that extended dance music by avoiding the usual pauses between songs. Parties were often spontaneous events; djs hooked their equipment to any electrical source, sometimes a hot-wired light fixture in an empty lot, and began to play music. Young people could dance continuously, a phoenix of pleasure among the ruins of the South Bronx.

Emcees came later, adding live rhymes to the music. Many lyrics in rap are about parties, love, hate, jewels, fast cars, alcohol, and drugs, but many of the artists create counter-narratives that contradict the dominant Eurocentric middle-class representations of the American dream. Two early rap songs exemplify the resistance and social commentary in the lyrics of hip hop. "The Message" by Grand Master Flash (1987/1994, track 4) was among the first to describe urban conditions and the resulting psychological strain. He raps, "Don't push me cause I'm close to the edge/I'm trying not to lose my head/It's like a jungle sometimes/Makes me wonder how I keep from going under." Run-D.M.C. (1984, track 7) expressed visions for a better world when they sang, "There were no street people, we live rent free/And every single person had a place to be/A job, a home, and the perfect pay/And the world was free of greed and hate." At the same time California rappers like Ice-T and N.W.A. (Niggaz with Attitude) searched for a rap style that represented them. Gangsta Rap was the outcome; songs like "Straight Outta Compton" (N.W.A., 1988) told the story of crime and urban warfare among gangs and with the police. "When I'm called off, I got a sawed off/Squeeze the trigger, and bodies are hauled off/You too, boy, if ya f**k with me/The police are gonna hafta come and get me."

Hip Hop as an Educational Tool

All these stories are available for interrogation through the techniques of critical media literacy. I use hip hop in teacher-education courses as an art form and as primary documents to be examined critically. Students create rap and spoken-word poetry and learn as audiences the power of hip hop to transform themselves and their students. Art helps us see the world differently, and hip hop art forms can be vehicles for creativity and reflection.

Reflection on Perceptions of Form and Assumptions. Jack Mezirow (1998) posits that "reflection, a 'turning back' on experience, can mean many things: simple awareness of an object, event or state, including awareness of a perception, thought, feeling, disposition, intention, action, or of one's habits of doing these things . . ." (p. 185). Percipience of art forms is a reflective practice that Eliot Eisner (2002) suggests stimulates affective modes of learning. He states that viewing the arts "requires a willingness to allow the form to inform the way we feel when we see it. Sight . . . is put in the service of feeling" (p. 86). Thus, the art experience is cognitive and emotional. John Dirkx (2006) points to the value of exploring emotions as a means of transformative learning. He states that emotional "dynamics suggest largely unconscious issues evoked by various aspects of the learning setting" (p. 17). Engaging mostly white teachers with African American hip hop artists requires a reflective process of questioning their assumptions in general and also their preconceptions about rap music, about the children and youth they teach, and particularly about the black male as a creative intellectual.

Certainly a contentious aspect of the topography of popular culture throughout the whole of the twentieth century is the contradictions raised by the African diasporic cultural presence in popular music. Black youth use creative symbolism (Willis, 1997) to construct a culture of language, behaviors, relationships, and commodities that counter the dominant discourse in schools and middle-class white communities on multiple levels. Unconscious and conscious fears of black males and the fear and shame of harboring those thoughts and feelings are reflected in many teachers' biases against rap and hip hop, about which they know little. I participated in a professional development project for teachers about curricular integration of musicians and musical forms found in the communities of the schools. Black and white teachers express amazement at the ability of black male emcees to command language, rhythm, rhyme, and complex concepts in an improvisational form known as freestyle. The emcee who performs freestyle takes words from the audience and improvises rhymes to beats often set by a dj. A good freestyler creates a tour de force of focus and literacy skill that transforms the perception of any person fortunate enough to be present. One teacher said about her experience in a hip hop workshop in which an African American emcee freestyled, "I had no idea how challenging rap could be, and how gifted the musicians are. I couldn't do what he did. . . . I can't think of anybody I know who could!"

One specific event is clear evidence of the transformative possibilities of immersion in hip hop. I took a small group of graduate students who were teachers and were preparing to be teacher educators to a hip hop workshop where an African American male emcee and an Asian American female dj taught a multiracial group of high school students about rap music. My goal was to get my students to think about black music as a means of culturally relevant instruction. The high school youngsters included the children of professionals as well as children of low-wealth workers. About a third of the high school students were black and on free and reduced-price lunches; they attended an alternative school for those who had been removed from their regular schools until they achieved stated academic or behavior goals. Assumptions about the abilities and behavior of these students and about hip hop were evident when one of the high school teachers from a predominantly middle-class and white school requested that her students not participate in the workshop.

The instructing emcee discussed rap as a form of poetry and listed attributes of poetry on the board: simile, metaphor, imagery, alliteration, assonance, consonance, onomatopoeia, meter, rhythm, and rhyme scheme. The students were asked the meaning of the words. One African American student from the alternative school who wore baggy and sagging pants and a do-rag and chewed on a toothpick knew the meaning of each of the terms. Later in the workshop he took words from participants and teachers and improvised poetry in rhythm and rhyme about the trials of being young and black in a white world and about boring education, wars, and corrupt politicians. He got a standing ovation from everyone.

The most profound part of this experience for me as an educator and the most germane to the subject of using an art form for transformative learning happened after the workshop. One of my graduate students came to me breathless with excitement. She told me she had wanted to speak to the young man who had freestyled, to tell him how impressed she was with his work, but she had been afraid. I asked her why she had been afraid. She replied, rather sheepishly, "I don't know. He's a black boy. . . . His rap was about racism and bad schools, and I'm a white teacher. . . ." Her voice trailed off. But, despite her fears, she had taken a deep breath and had told him how wonderful she thought his poetry was. Then she smiled and said,

New Directions for Adult and Continuing Education • DOI: 10.1002/ace

"And he *hugged* me! And then I told him how impressed I was by his performance and freestyle—and he hugged me again!" She was transformed by this experience because she had to confront her assumptions and feelings about this black male, his abilities, and responses. Mezirow (1998) asserts that "critical reflection may be either implicit, as when we mindlessly choose between good and evil because of our assimilated values, or explicit, as when we bring the process of choice into awareness to examine and assess the reasons for making a choice" (p. 185). My unplanned question about her trepidations put her in a reflective stance that required an open and critical assessment of her fears and assumptions.

An art that contests the dominant culture of racism through an Afrocentric form but represents the black experience with drugs, violence, and misogyny is replete with opportunities for critical literacy. Almost any question asked about rap or hip hop can lead to a heated debate. After an open mic in a black-owned coffeehouse before an audience of adolescents and young adults, some of whom were my graduate students, the emcees turned on the lights and began to converse with the audience. They discussed the forms of rap—freestyle and battling—a form of verbal competition in which two emcees exchange insults with wit and rhyme for audiences, and they talked about effective open-mic techniques. I asked this group of mostly African Americans, "Since there is so much disrespect of black women in many rap songs, what meaning does that have for the future of the black family and community?" The discussion of that one question lasted more than an hour. There were arguments about freedom of creativity and censorship and about the representations of black women in rap being just another variation of the racist depictions whites perpetuated in films in the pre–civil rights era. One young woman said, "You know what? You're talking about violence toward half of our people, and we're the ones who do a lot of raising the children. We're the ones who are your mamas and will be your daughters when you have them—if you don't already. How are you going to hurt us like that and expect our people to be strong?" One teenage male said, "It's just music. . ." Before he could finish his thought both male and female audience members erupted in response about the power of music to teach. They challenged each other's frames of reference and had to defend their perspectives to the community members present. Emotion played a major part in the process. More than one of the emcees and audience members edged away from unexamined positions.

Creation of Hip Hop Forms. Creating art is a process of transforming material, perspectives, and concepts. Eisner (1980) describes the processes of creation as perception, conceptualization, expression, and transformation. An artist must shape meaning in a medium and yield to its idiosyncrasies. Hence, self-expression is a reflective process that connects cognition and affective and intuitive knowing. It also involves imagination, creativity, cultural knowledge, expressiveness, and skills in observation, sensory awareness, problem solving, hypothesizing, risk taking, decision making, focus and concentration, and patterning. I have used the creative process of writing and performing at an open mic in my arts-integration classrooms for preservice teachers to demonstrate the possibilities of using popular culture to teach children. However, my prime objectives are to encourage these undergraduate students to experience the creative process with the reflection, vulnerability, emotion, and conceptualization that goes with it and to build a community of adult learners and artists. I have also been amazed at what I learn about student perspectives and cultures from listening to their creative work. Jackie Davis-Manigaulte, Lyle York, and Elizabeth Kasl (2006) underscore this observation as they use expressive ways of knowing to encourage transformative learning. They found that students developed empathy through sharing their art works, and I find that such empathy builds a sense of community in the classroom.

Spoken-word poetry, often heard at open-mic performances, has its roots in the Beat poets of the 1940s–1950s and in performance groups like the Last Poets in the 1970s; it intersects with the literary and performance art of hip hop as well as with the counter-narratives of the youth who claim to speak truth to power. Unlike commercial rap lyrics, spoken word often does not rhyme, and more than some rap songs spoken word often includes critical commentary on social issues.

The open-mic technique I use I learned about in one of my forays into the sites of hip hop. I attended an open mic in a coffeehouse. The youngest participant was five years old; there were also six black and white men and women between forty and sixty years of age. Most people in the audience were in their late teens to middle thirties. The first part of the open mic was a free-write period in which three words were taken from the audience of African, Asian, Native, Latino, and European Americans. Everyone was given twenty minutes to write poetry using the three suggested words. Then people were encouraged to read their work by hand clapping, foot stomping, laughter, and cheers, and such phrases as "Everybody, show them some love"; "Let's clap till they get up here! Make some noise!" "I know you have something wonderful to share with us. Don't be shy!" No criticism was allowed, only positive support for the writing and performance. The effect was moving and engrossing. A room of about seventy-five people from diverse backgrounds developed an empathic relationship. An eight-year-old African American girl read her poem and encouraged her mother and father to read. Even the five-year-old Latino boy drew a picture about the words. His sister translated its meaning to the gathering. The poets made themselves vulnerable and presented long and short poems, some funny, some sad, some with rhyme and rhythm, some in free verse, some rather trite, others challenging form or raising critical questions about society and social justice. Whatever was offered was welcomed and applauded. The second half of the open mic was devoted to the reading of poetry that people had

New Directions for Adult and Continuing Education • DOI: 10.1002/ace

written before that evening. Again the emphasis was on sharing and acknowledging the work of creativity.

In using this open-mic event with my students I use a plastic microphone or even a broom handle. The effect of the performance does not have the same focus without the prop, and people talk into the "mic" as though it were real even though they have the option to read without it. We use dictionaries, thesauruses, and rhyming dictionaries for those who want to use rhyme in their poetry. I have often served as the emcee to model the necessary style of energy and welcome. I have recently invited students to emcee and have found that some consider themselves to be emcees or hip hop lyricists. As a result, I have learned about my students in ways I would not have otherwise.

I share myself as well. I read whatever I have written in the twenty-minute free-write period. I've learned firsthand the vulnerability that goes with sharing unedited work and the appreciation for the applause. There are often miles of knowing between a professor and students and, in this case, between a black professor and white students. I cross a generational and cultural border to share a hip hop space with my mostly white and female students; this sharing connects to my own "old school" experience as an African American writer and performer—and former young adult. The creative process allows us to share our cultural selves and to represent our identities and our common struggle for voice and meaning-making. When we listen to our poetic stories, we learn to read the world through differences in form and content. Writing and performance provide a bridge to multiple meanings, and literacy becomes a means of being relevant and part of a dialogue that welcomes difference.

Students also learn about themselves and their teaching as we reflect on the event. We discuss their strengths and fears about self-expression, performance, and community building and probe the influences on their thinking and teaching. This work also provides an alternative form of instruction for students experienced with what Paulo Freire (1970) calls the "banking method" of teaching, wherein students are treated as passive containers who receive, rather than interact with or transform, knowledge. The open mic creates ruptures in the notions of what is appropriate in classrooms and increases the possibility of transformation.

Conclusion

Across the United States thousands of adult learners of all ethnicities and social classes are engaged in the social construction of meaning through music and culture. John Dewey (1934) maintained that humans create art forms in order to find harmony and equilibrium in a world of chaos. The late twentieth century was certainly a complex era, and nothing in the new millennium suggests that experience will get simpler. Hip hop culture promotes

New Directions for Adult and Continuing Education • DOI: 10.1002/ace

expressions of the pain and pleasures of the generation born after the cultural revolution of the 1960s and 1970s, a time when postmodern identity politics competes with a modernist ideology of social justice, and consumption threatens to overstretch the earth's resources. Making sense of the chaos is for adult learners an enormous task that the creation and perception of the art forms of hip hop can help to clarify. Educators of adults who use hip hop in their classrooms can engage students in critical thought while they incorporate the learner-centered processes inherent in creating the arts.

Whole-person learning that connects rationality, emotion, and intuition provides multiple avenues for sense making. The comfort of an empathetic community, in spite or because of its diversity, supports reflection and the interrogation of meaning and opens border crossings for teachers and students to experience interchangeable roles. Using the culture of adult learners as the form and content of the curriculum addresses the first rule of good teaching: start with the knowledge of the learner. However, to effectively use hip hop an educator must do the research so that the culture is authentically represented; even if students bring knowledge, an educator who is uninformed can bring little to the table at the crossroads.

References

Davis-Manigaulte, J., York, L., and Kasl, E. "Expressive Ways of Knowing and Transformative Learning." In E. Taylor (ed.), *Teaching for Change: Fostering Transformative Learning in the Classroom*. New Directions for Adult and Continuing Education, no. 109. San Francisco: Jossey-Bass, 2006.

Dewey, J. *Art as Experience*. New York: Penguin Books, 1934.

Dirkx, J. M. "Engaging Emotions in Adult Learning: A Jungian Perspective on Emotion and Transformative Learning." In E. Taylor (ed.), *Teaching for Change: Fostering Transformative Learning in the Classroom*. New Directions for Adult and Continuing Education, no. 109. San Francisco: Jossey-Bass, 2006.

Eisner, E. "Artistic Thinking, Human Intelligence and the Mission of the School." *High School Journal*, 1980, *63*(8), 326–334.

Eisner, E. *The Arts and the Creation of Mind*. New Haven, Conn.: Yale University Press, 2002.

Freire, P. *Pedagogy of the Oppressed*. New York: Herder and Herder, 1970.

George, N. *Hip Hop America*. New York: Viking Penguin, 1998.

Grandmaster Flash. "The Message." On the compact disc *Ba-dop-boom-bang*. Elecktra Entertainment Group, 1987.

Guy, T. C. "Gangsta Rap and Adult Education." In L. Martin and E. Rogers (eds.), *Adult Education in an Urban Context*. New Directions for Adult and Continuing Education, no. 101. San Francisco, Jossey-Bass, 2004.

Mezirow, J. "On Critical Reflection." *Adult Education Quarterly*, 1998, *48*(3), 185–198.

Morrell, E. "Toward a Critical Pedagogy of Popular Culture: Literacy Development Among Urban Youth." *Journal of Adolescent and Adult Literacy*, 2002, *46*(1), 72–77.

N.W.A. (Niggaz with Attitude). "Straight Outta Compton." On the compact disc *Straight Outta Compton*. Priority Records, 1988.

Ogg, A., and Upshal, D. *The Hip Hop Years: A History of Rap*. New York: Fromm International, 2001.

Price, J. P. "Hegemony, Hope, and the Harlem Renaissance: Taking Hip Hop Culture Seriously." *Convergence,* 2005, *33*(2), 55–64.

Rose, T. *Black Noise: Rap Music and Black Culture in Contemporary America.* Middletown, Conn.: Wesleyan University Press, 1994.

Run-D.M.C. "Wake Up." On the compact disc *Run-D.M.C.* Profile Records, 1984.

Willis, P. "Symbolic Creativity." In A. Gray and J. McGuigan (eds.), *Studying Culture: An Introductory Reader.* London: Arnold, 1997.

MARY STONE HANLEY is assistant professor of education at George Mason University.

New Directions for Adult and Continuing Education • DOI: 10.1002/ace

5

This chapter discusses how the animated show The Simpsons *can be used successfully to present and critique various concepts normally found in traditional undergraduate Humanities courses.*

Using *The Simpsons* to Teach Humanities with Gen X and Gen Y Adult Students

Maxwell A. Fink, Deborah C. Foote

Media have a powerful influence in all of our lives. Many educators lament the UNESCO study showing that by the time the average teen graduates from high school he or she has spent more than fifteen thousand hours watching television and only eleven thousand in the classroom (Gorebel, 1998). Rather than regretting this "condition," colleges, universities, and educators of adults and children should recognize it as an opportunity. More than ever, educators can successfully incorporate media studies into existing courses and curricula and utilize this general experience of their student populations. Perhaps no show lends itself more to such an academic endeavor than the Fox network's mega-hit *The Simpsons*. Year after year, *The Simpsons* extends its reign as the longest running U.S. sitcom and the longest running U.S. animated television program of all time (McAllister, n.d.). It also is a cultural, economic, and global reference. *The Simpsons* can go beyond its extremely entertaining two-dimensional depictions to address critical and sophisticated issues often introduced and presented in the college classroom.

The two of us co-authors teach undergraduate Humanities courses in which the majority of our students are members of Generation X (those born between 1963 and 1977) or older members of Generation Y (born after 1977). Most of them are as familiar with *The Simpsons* as the boomers are with *Leave It to Beaver.* It is therefore easy to engage them in discussions of

some of the themes depicted on *The Simpsons,* many of which are also themes presented in Humanities classes.

In this chapter, we each briefly discuss how we got interested in *The Simpsons,* particularly in using it for teaching purposes. Next, we consider media theories that suggest how *The Simpsons* works to critique and satirize our cultural condition. Finally, we each describe how we draw on *The Simpsons* in our educational practices.

Who We Are and Why We Love *The Simpsons*

Each of us is a strong fan of *The Simpsons* and draws on it in our practice, though in different ways. Here we speak in separate voices to describe how we came to use *The Simpsons* in our classes.

Max Fink. Until I agreed to take part in the writing of this chapter, I had never thought of my love for *The Simpsons* in the context of my status as a Gen Xer. Most of my classmates and I rejected the Ronald Reagan–era ethos of our early teenage years, but we viewed hippies and yuppies with equal skepticism. Although *The Simpsons* first appeared on television scarcely a year after the final days of the Reagan presidency, I somehow barely noticed the show until around the time when the term *Generation X* was first coined. I realize now that the convergence of these two occasions was no mere coincidence.

I can see clearly now how the traits that qualify me as a Gen Xer are the same qualities that make me such a huge fan of *The Simpsons* and an even bigger fan of the critical mind-set inspired by the show since the dawn of that generational era. My sense of humor, like that of the *Simpsons* creators, is based on an even mix of cynicism and idealism. My outlook on the world and on life is never too serious, but like the outlook of the show it often reveals a great deal about the most serious issues in life.

Just as *The Simpsons* defies categorization while playing many different social roles, I seek ways in which critical examples of popular culture like *The Simpsons* itself can be used as versatile teaching tools to increase social awareness in a variety of different adult education contexts and particularly within my own setting as a community college English instructor.

Deb Foote. Unlike most fellow Gen Xers and *Simpsons* fans, my interest in the show did not emerge until my early days of graduate school, seven years after the program had established itself as a cultural phenomenon and possible social threat. Through my years as a part-time instructor in various undergraduate Humanities classes, I noticed many themes presented in the required heavy textbooks and seemingly cumbersome primary texts. When I received my current position as a full-time lecturer at Columbia College Chicago, I did not realize the full significance that teaching languages and Humanities at one of the largest and most diverse private arts and media colleges in the United States would carry. Finding myself in classrooms with

New Directions for Adult and Continuing Education • DOI: 10.1002/ace

primarily film, television, radio, and animation majors changed the ways in which I related to and communicated with my students. No matter where I taught at various colleges and universities across Chicago, though, whether as a graduate student, part-time instructor, or full-time lecturer, the one constant I found was Fox's popular Sunday night animation show. My realization of the show's popularity prompted me to propose and then to teach a class entitled *The Simpsons* as Satirical Authors.

Theorizing *The Simpsons* and Why It Works

Before discussing how we draw on *The Simpsons* in our respective practices, we consider why *The Simpsons* works as a cultural phenomenon and how it can be used as an analytical tool in cultural studies and in humanities. Three major theoretical areas offer some explanation: *The Simpsons* as "oppositional culture," *The Simpsons* as a blend of (and a critique of) both "high" and "low" culture, and the uniquely critical use of stereotypes on *The Simpsons*.

The Simpsons as Oppositional Culture.   The use of *The Simpsons* for analyzing social issues in educational settings is rooted in a theoretical framework of critical media literacy, which extends the focus of critical theory from the structure of social power to the news and entertainment media and how they are produced and consumed (Alvermann and others, 1999). One can also view critical awareness of media power as a form of "conscientization," or the process by which critical viewers realize their roles in communal efforts for positive social change (Freire, [1971] 2000). As John Alberti (2004) notes, critical awareness functions as oppositional culture, which essentially means that we can analyze *The Simpsons* to understand what it is saying about social issues.

"But it's just a cartoon," you might respond, and you'd hardly be alone in that sentiment. However, any self-respecting *Simpsons* fan can tell you that in part such cultural underestimation has allowed the show to be the consistent critical force it has been for so long. Alberti (2004) notes that "a key attraction for many fans of the show has been the sense of 'getting away with something.'. . . *The Simpsons* has entered fully into the mainstream, even while apparently embracing ideas (e.g., the promotion of paganism; the critique of Christianity) that conventional wisdom would see as fatal to mass public acceptance" (p. xii). *The Simpsons* also maintains its oppositional powers within the mainstream segment of our culture by constantly shifting perspective; it makes fun of one social group while winking at another, and then may reverse that approach later on. This is a point Paul Armstrong (2005) also makes when discussing the role of *The Simpsons* as political satire in adult education: the writers poke fun at the Democrats and the Republicans alike. When interviewed on the subject, *Simpsons* creator Matt Groening has said, "It's always fun—kids know this—to tell a joke that makes all the kids laugh but which confuses and annoys the teacher. And that's what I try to do as a grown-up—entertain part of the audience and annoy the other part" (quoted in Angel, 1993, p. 23). Perhaps because the writers annoy viewers on different ends of the political spectrum, *The Simpsons* gets away with plots and characterizations that other shows can't get away with; to watch the show in a socially critical way requires a silent agreement by the viewer to respect the double-edged aspects of the show and its audience.

The Simpsons as Carnival.   For those of us who view and use *The Simpsons* in a critical way, a good point of comparison is the commentary by Mikhail Bakhtin (1984) on Rabelais's literary vision of the medieval carnival and on why carnival works. Carnival was a nonconformist segment of medieval society; it was a free, expressive cultural response and alternative to the repressive aspects of the dominant overall culture of the time. Bakhtin describes carnival as a "temporary liberation from the prevailing truth and from the established order; it marked the suspension of all hierarchical rank, privileges, norms and prohibitions" (p. 10). In its democratic approach to humor (in the sense of poking fun at all sides) and its consistent challenging of what most people accept as normal, *The Simpsons* vividly reflects the spirit of the carnival. And, yes, even in sight gags featuring Homer's exposed butt cheeks, the critical truth of carnival's "grotesque realism" is hard at work (Rhodes, 2001).

Another interesting parallel between *The Simpsons* and carnival is that both phenomena represent critical intersections between "high" and "low" culture. Although carnival was a kind of cultural valve that tempered people's appetites and tolerances for the absolute extreme forms of the two, *The Simpsons* provides a cultural measurement of the gap between those extremes (Arnold, 2004, p. 2). In the process, the show pokes plenty of fun at both sides in a way that exposes the role each one plays in reinforcing social hegemony. Take the diametrically opposed examples of the villainous Sideshow Bob, who is such a vehement defender of high culture that he tries to take television away from all of Springfield, and of Bart Simpson, who wants no part of any educational activity that doesn't come in video-game form. Do Gen X and Gen Y students identify closely with Bart's slacker mentality because they share the same rejection of previous generations' values, which have in many ways not lived up to their promise? Perhaps the answers to such questions lie in a critical examination of shows like *The Simpsons* and how they reflect and affect our culture.

Use of Stereotypes on The Simpsons.   Though *The Simpsons* has come under fire from various interest groups for its heavy use of stereotypes, the show's employment of this technique can be seen through critical eyes as much more than a hackneyed try for cheap laughs at the expense of the already-victimized.

One of the principal ways in which *The Simpsons* may be considered "oppositional" is through its use of pre-existing mass media stereotypes precisely in order to destabilize them. . . . The members of the Simpson family themselves conform to a particular popular conception of "the American family.". . . Many characters' clichéd characteristics serve not only as a means to critique elements of American society that are seen to have become stereotypical, but also as a method of undermining the perceived validity of the bland, two-dimensional views of American national identity presented by the mainstream mass media. [Beard, 2004, pp. 273–274]

In this way, *The Simpsons* shifts the critical focus away from the oft-oppressed victims of stereotypes and places it on the power of dominant cultural influences, particularly those responsible for disseminating information. This kind of focus is also applied to the specific ethnic stereotypes that are so pervasive in news and entertainment media.

Apu is one *Simpsons* character who shows us how superficial stereotypes can be combined with other personality traits to critique the origins, motivations, and deceptions behind those images. He is an Indian American immigrant who stretches the seams of many common stereotypes while blatantly defying others. Because many of the Gen Xers and Gen Yers that we know share a postmodern tendency to eschew social labels and preconceived notions about people, this critical use of stereotypes on *The Simpsons* makes it a useful example of critical media literacy at work within the media mainstream that both the show itself and the theoretical framework attempt to critique. At least we attempt to use the show's stereotyping in this way.

Using *The Simpsons* in Our Teaching Practice

As noted, both of us teach Humanities classes, but each of us teaches different classes, and thus we use *The Simpsons* in different ways. Here, each of us describes how we use the show in practice.

Deb Foote's Class. For many of the reasons noted above in discussing the theories about why *The Simpsons* works, I proposed, created, and received approval for a course entitled *The Simpsons* as Satirical Authors. In the course rationale, I specified that the class would present various disciplines within the humanities and analyze how they portray and critique various themes and representations. Course objectives focused on self-representation, self-reference, distinctions between high and low art, and examination of the advantages and disadvantages of popular mass culture within the context of postmodernity. The first syllabus also included a detailed course outline that explained and justified how studies in popular culture can facilitate discussions normally reserved for classes focused on high art and high culture. Discussion topics centered on socially

New Directions for Adult and Continuing Education • DOI: 10.1002/ace

"subversive" identities like the elderly, gay/lesbian/ transgender individuals, and proponents of civil disobedience in the United States.

As the course creator and instructor, I chose these themes and episodes subjectively, based on my own experiences of (at the time the syllabus was originally proposed) fifteen seasons of *The Simpsons*. Course readings include several books that discuss various approaches to *The Simpsons* as an influential cultural trend in the United States. Although *The Simpsons* animation series is the main "text" for this class, it is supplemented by Alberti's *Leaving Springfield: The Simpsons and the Possibility of Oppositional Culture* (2004). To avoid the many obvious issues that might arise from asking my students to purchase or borrow the DVD copies of the *Simpsons* episodes to be discussed in class, I offer the class over the fifteen-week semester approximately three hours a week, one hour for watching the two twenty-three-minute episodes and two hours for discussion, class presentations, and other activities.

Evaluation of students occurs on several levels, as specified by the course syllabus. Class attendance and active participation in classroom discussions are among the students' responsibilities, along with the weekly chapter readings from *Leaving Springfield*. A midterm asks students to summarize the terminology and episodes presented in class and to discuss the importance of the selection to and within this Humanities/cultural studies class. Students must also answer an essay question using both supporting evidence from class and course readings and their own thoughtful, meaningful observations. Based on classroom discussions of episodes, they must summarize an episode they chose and analyze the contributions it makes to humanities or cultural studies or both. Finally, students must successfully complete a take-home final exam in which they again must define terms and theoretical concepts by using examples from one *Simpsons* episode not shown in class.

The effectiveness of this course far exceeds all expectations during its creation. The biggest concern when proposing this class centered on student perceptions and abilities: Would students approach this course simply as a fan club, or would they rise to the challenge and see *The Simpsons* with an academic eye for multiple interpretations?

Several factors contribute to the success of this course and its popularity, especially among students of Gen X and Gen Y. Most significantly, the exposure to *The Simpsons* that students have before entering the classroom and arguably before entering higher education, whether significant or not, contributes directly to their success in the classroom. It lessens the potentially intimidating traditional structure of the classroom environment. Such students are more likely to participate, ask and answer questions, and engage with the class material than are students who are completely unaware of or have little knowledge of *The Simpsons*. For these students the risk of participation may remain the same as in other classes, but using the medium of animation also lessens the intimidation factor that is present when students are expected to appreciate and analyze traditional forms of representation and expression.

Aside from issues related to authority and confidence, the class also encourages student participation and engagement because it is concerned with portrayals normally deemed unacceptable and insensitive in nonanimated mediums. Not only do animated series more easily introduce and utilize a wider variety of characters than shows with "real" human characters, but these characters also can more easily represent beliefs, behaviors, and ideas—both positive and negative. Primary characters like Homer and Bart Simpson, secondary characters like Mr. Burns and Chief Clancy Wiggum, and even peripheral characters like fourth-grade teacher Edna Krabappel and attorney Lionel Hutz all have skewed and exaggerated views on such controversial subjects as immigration, dating and marriage, unemployment, and parental responsibility. Although animation allows its characters more skewed and unenlightened behavior without any significant or realistic penalties than does nonanimation, it also creates a space where multiple sides of an issue can be generalized and presented quickly. When all sides are represented, students can see the distinct arguments, formulate their own interpretations, and participate accordingly.

And they do participate. Unlike other Humanities courses that I've taught, this course elicits so much participation that I cannot keep up with the raised hands and the voices of students who have something to say. Furthermore, student preparation for class seems significantly higher in this course than in others, and I receive homework assignments in a more timely manner and with a generally higher level of thought and analysis. Although other factors may contribute to these findings, utilizing *The Simpsons* and students' television-viewing habits in general may indicate a postmodern change in our classrooms and pedagogical techniques in ways that empower and engage students rather than intimidate and bore them.

Max Fink's Practice. I am an adult education doctoral student whose dissertation (in process) is on the use of *The Simpsons* in teaching Humanities. I have begun to consider how *The Simpsons* might serve as a rich resource within my own undergraduate community college classroom. I teach English to students who are mostly members of Gen X and Gen Y. These students look to me for guidance in improving their expressive skills through formal writing instruction and in improving their critical-thinking skills through thematic analysis of literature. However, I also feel that it is my responsibility to tell my students that these skills are of little use or consequence without a keen awareness of the social contexts in which they will be used. For this reason I think that an understanding of critical media literacy is essential to the practical application of the subject matter I teach.

A great number of the main themes or underlying intended messages within many significant works of literature are based on power and its effects on social relationships. Such themes and the characters and plots that illustrate them can be viewed as parallels to the philosophy of critical media literacy in that they caution us against the abuse of social power. Because *The Simpsons* is such a prominent yet subversive representation of so many aspects of popular culture, it is an effective tool in helping students make these thematic connections and apply them to their own lives.

One classic tale of a social power structure gone awry is a short story by Shirley Jackson (2005) entitled "The Lottery," first published in 1948. In it an insular community holds a lottery drawing to decide who will be the next victim of routine public executions by stoning. These rituals are performed partly for the entertainment of the masses and partly to remind the masses of the limits to their power, but mostly out of a blind sense of duty and tradition (despite a general ignorance of the reasons behind the traditions). This fictional social structure illustrates the problems that can arise from the misuse of power.

These thematic connections are illustrated particularly well in one *Simpsons* episode in which "The Lottery" is referred to directly. During the chaos spurred by an unusually high lottery jackpot, Springfield TV anchorman Kent Brockman attempts to calm the masses by assuring them that Jackson's story has nothing to do with winning *that* kind of lottery and that they should therefore cease their rampant trashing of libraries and bookstores in search of it. Though Jackson's story has little to do with hitting the jackpot, the riotous Springfield mob bent on winning obscene amounts of cash at the expense of public safety is quite similar to Jackson's mob in a thematic sense: both mobs sacrifice their dignity and self-control in an attempt to satisfy base human urges.

The lottery-related *Simpsons* video clip could be used as part of a lecture and discussion lesson in courses such as mine to display how themes from both classic literature and contemporary entertainment media can heighten learners' awareness of critical media literacy and the impact the media have on their lives. Other *Simpsons* clips show similar thematic connections without the direct literary references of the lottery episode. In this way, *The Simpsons* can provide many modern, accessible, versatile, memorable, and entertaining representations of connected social and literary themes of power that are directly relevant to adult students' experiences.

Conclusion

Through our exploration of the ways in which *The Simpsons* can be used in higher education contexts to teach undergraduate Gen X and Gen Y students, we have both found many common themes to be true. For example, we have learned that the show can reinforce class lessons by illustrating key concepts in humorous, entertaining, unique, and interesting ways. Because

The Simpsons is largely a phenomenon of the Gen X and Gen Y eras of popular culture, it often critically reflects recent events that continue to shape the future for members of those generations.

The show is also an appropriate tool for the study of the media's connection to social themes because the show deals with such a broad variety of subject matter that is relevant to our culture. Much like the philosophy of critical media literacy itself, *The Simpsons* seeks to present information in the most democratic possible way by encouraging critical thought and thus empowering audience members to reach their own conclusions about how certain social issues might affect them or those around them. The motivations behind the creation of *The Simpsons* also are akin to the principles of critical media literacy in that they are peacefully subversive of many of the most harmful (and most widely accepted) abuses of power in society.

The postmodern nature of *The Simpsons* makes it an ideal springboard for discussion among Gen X and Gen Y students who are able to transcend the false labels and categories that have tended to limit the scope of social debate in the past. Finally, and perhaps most important overall, *The Simpsons* can be used to show these students that both high and low culture are of special value as tools for learning and that both are thematically connected and thus can and should be studied together in many cases.

References

Alberti, J. (ed.). *Leaving Springfield:* The Simpsons *and the Possibility of Oppositional Culture.* Detroit: Wayne State University Press, 2004.

Alvermann, D. E., and others. *Popular Culture in the Classroom: Teaching and Researching Critical Media Literacy.* Mahwah, N.J.: LEA, 1999.

Angel, J. A. "Explaining Groening: One on One with the Sultan of Fun." *Simpsons Illustrated,* 1993, *1*(9), 22–30.

Armstrong, P. "*The Simpsons* and Democracy: Political Apathy, Popular Culture, and Lifelong Learning as Satire." In R. Hill and R. Kiely (eds.), *Proceedings of the 46th Annual Adult Education Research Conference.* Athens: University of Georgia, 2005.

Arnold, D. G. "Use a Pen, Sideshow Bob: *The Simpsons* and the Threat of High Culture." In J. Alberti (ed.), *Leaving Springfield:* The Simpsons *and the Possibility of Oppositional Culture.* Detroit: Wayne State University Press, 2004.

Bakhtin, M. M. *Rabelais and His World* (H. Iswolsky, trans.). Bloomington: Indiana University Press, 1984.

Beard, D. S. "Local Satire with a Global Reach: Ethnic Stereotyping and Cross-Cultural Conflicts in *The Simpsons.*" In J. Alberti (ed.), *Leaving Springfield:* The Simpsons *and the Possibility of Oppositional Culture.* Detroit: Wayne State University Press, 2004.

Freire, P. *Pedagogy of the Oppressed.* New York: Continuum, 2000. (Originally published 1971.)

Gans, H. *Popular Culture and High Culture: An Analysis and Evolution of Taste.* New York: Basic Books, 1999.

Gorebel, J. "The UNESCO Global Study on Media Violence." In *Children and Media Violence: Yearbook from the International Clearinghouse on Children and Media Violence on the Screen.* Goteberg, Sweden: UNESCO, 1998.

Jackson, S. *The Lottery and Other Stories.* New York: Farrar, Straus & Giroux, 2005.

McAllister, M. n.d. Retrieved from www.museum.tv/archives/etv/S/htmlS/simpsons-the/simpsonsthe.htm.

Rhodes, C. "D'oh: *The Simpsons,* Popular Culture, and the Organizational Carnival." *Journal of Management Inquiry,* 2001, *10*(4), 374–383.

MAXWELL A. FINK *is a doctoral candidate in adult education at the Pennsylvania State University, Harrisburg, and adjunct instructor of English at Anne Arundel Community College.*

DEBORAH C. FOOTE *is the foreign-languages coordinator at Columbia College Chicago and a graduate student in Romance languages and literatures (Spanish) at the University of Chicago.*

6

This chapter focuses on the informal use of popular media by literacy workers to open up new possibilities for building literacy.

Using Popular Media to Build Literacy

Barbara P. Heuer

When an adult student from China says he learned English from listening to the radio or a literacy teacher mentions that she is reading a book recommended on *Oprah*, they are illustrating how popular media are used for informal adult learning. This chapter examines some of the issues and implications surrounding how a sector of adult learners, literacy teachers and their students, use popular media in the form of television, videos, and magazines to build literacy.

Popular media are omnipresent messengers and conduits of popular culture. As the sociologist David Riesman (1950) observed, "By its very nature, popular culture impinges on people unceasingly; it is part of their environment, part of the background noise, color and verbal imagery of their lives from the age at which they can listen to the radio, watch television . . . [or read comics]. My judgment is that the same or virtually the same popular culture materials are used by audiences in radically different ways and for radically different purposes" (p. 359).

With the vast accessibility to mass media in the form of television, radio, video, magazines, and newspapers, most adults in the United States have regular media-usage habits. One survey estimates that in the United States most people get their news from television, listen to the radio over two hours daily, and spend forty-five minutes reading a daily newspaper (Tait, 2004). This usage pattern reaches across socioeconomic, ethnic, and cultural lines. These media are available and accessible at the lowest end of the socioeconomic scale. Television, radio, magazines, and newspapers are delivering sounds, voices, images, and print to entertain and inform (and sell) daily.

NEW DIRECTIONS FOR ADULT AND CONTINUING EDUCATION, no. 115, Fall 2007 © 2007 Wiley Periodicals, Inc.
Published online in Wiley InterScience (www.interscience.wiley.com) • DOI: 10.1002/ace.267

Informal learning and its corollary, incidental learning, are the predominant forms of adult learning (Marsick and Watkins, 2001). Adults choose what, where, and how they will learn and usually are the evaluators of their own learning. Although the adult education literature emphasizes the crucial role the adult learner's context plays in informal learning, an almost universal element of that context, mass media, and their connection to learning have been little researched (Lewis, 1982).

The omnipresence of the media in people's lives and their use of them to learn informally came to my attention when I was involved in conducting a series of professional workshops for literacy teachers. The other professional developers on the team and I saw how readily and familiarly the literacy workers engaged with media in the workshops. We wondered whether and how they and their students also used mass media to learn informally outside the classroom. The purpose of this chapter is to explore how media are used by adult-literacy learners, and how they can be used in facilitating the development of adult literacy. In order to properly set the context, I first discuss conceptualizations of literacy education and media. Next, I discuss some examples from my own practice about the way media-usage habits can be used to facilitate the development of literacy. I end with some conclusions for practice.

Popular Media and Adult Literacy: Conceptual Perspectives

Until recently, the informal use of mass media by adult nonreaders has rarely been explored. Surveys of adult literacy have provided statistics on the attrition rates, race, gender, ethnicity, and education level of adults in literacy programs (Beder and Medina, 1999; Kaestle and others, 2001). Few surveys mention the resources adults use to become literate. An ethnographic study started by the Center for Literacy Studies in which immigrant workers in Appalachia and California were interviewed reported that the workers' regular media-usage habits included reading a daily newspaper and watching television for news, information, and entertainment (Merrifield, Bingman, Hemphill, and deMarais, 1995). Maurice Taylor's (2006) study in Canada of informal learning practices found that adults with limited literacy skills engaged in everyday literacy activities connected to their roles at home, in the community, and at work. Participants in the study used radio and television to gather information that they then applied "in their own way in their own time" (p. 505).

Two perspectives have hampered recognition of media's role in informally fostering literacy. One centers on the developing definitions of literacy. The other is a suspicion of the educative abilities of mass media. Traditional definitions of literacy have provided little space for media's informal role. The classic basis of literacy has been the written word, and literacy implies having the decoding skills to recognize letters, words, their sounds, and

New Directions for Adult and Continuing Education • DOI: 10.1002/ace

their meanings. This "autonomous" model (Street, 2001, p. 14) understands literacy to be a set of linguistic skills independent of context and, to some degree, has been the main focus for most adult-literacy programs and their assessments. This definition of literacy implies a correct, measurable set of decoding skills. The adult student who lacks skills and knowledge according to these established standards represents the "deficit" model (Quigley, 1997) and needs to be brought up to a certain level of linguistic and numeracy competence as measured by standardized tests like the GED or TABE. From this standpoint, the learner's context, which may include media-usage habits, is irrelevant.

A broader definition has developed that understands literacy as a social practice intimately interwoven with the learners' culture, community, and history (Taylor, 2006). "This view of literacy moves beyond skills and tasks to recognize the role of meaning and context explicitly" (Fingeret and Drennon, 1997, p. 63). This "relational" definition implies that literacy is the ability to make meaning from and to interpret resources and relationships in one's environment. "New" literacy studies further delineate perspectives of literacy as functional, liberal, and radical/critical, in which "literacy is studied in the social/cultural, political and economic practices of which they are a part" (Holland, 1998, p. 13). This definition of literacy accommodates not only different, specially focused literacies like information literacy and family literacy but also the evaluative and reflective aspects of critical media literacy. This contextualized definition makes room for an understanding of the nonreader's broad coping skills (Fingeret, 1993) and acknowledges how adult nonreaders have worked, parented, and otherwise led their lives without being able to read. This constructivist stance is interested in the adult's habits, experiences, and already-in-place fluencies as a bridge to new understandings. These adult-role competencies include informal media-usage habits.

The second conceptual issue around adult literacy and popular media is the perception that radio and television are antithetical to learning because of their content and delivery format. A presentation at a Toronto conference of literacy and media experts (Centre for Literacy, 2000) captured this long-held sentiment about popular media and adult literacy. As pointed out in this session, television, while omnipresent in North American households, was little considered or was soundly criticized as a tool for developing adult literacy on the basis that technologies like radio and television provide entertainment, not education. "Consuming popular media has often been seen as requiring no intellectual competences and thus [the tendency is] to develop none" (Buckingham and Sefton-Green, 1994, p. 21). Another education expert states that most teachers of literacy have viewed television as the enemy (Singh, 2000, p. 16).

One can point to many successful examples of educational programming and articles specifically for adult learners on television, on the radio, and in newspapers. Intentional use of the media through educational programming, although not the emphasis in this chapter, has often been tailored to adult learning and has attractive features (Bates, 1990) like its entertainment value and pace. One example, TV411, demonstrates the learning dimensions of media: their relevance, resources, and visual aspects. Developed by the Adult Literacy Media Alliance, TV411 is a TV- and video-based national literacy service organized around three themes important to adults—parenting, money, and health. "Television and video expand a teacher's resources, making it possible to bring celebrity speakers, adult-learner role models, and real-life contexts, such as looking under the hood of a car, into the classroom. These media also make it possible to use graphics and animation to explain complex concepts and to comfortably visit and experience such literacy rich settings as bookstores and libraries" (Donnelly, 2000, p. 27). Adult-learning principles that emphasize relevance, practicality, learner readiness, and past experiences as well as the importance of social and cultural context suggest the need to tap into the learner's media-usage habits. But the linguistic-skills-only definition of literacy and the idea that television is simply passive entertainment may have clouded the lens through which we see how media has been and can be informally used in building literacy.

Tapping Popular Media to Facilitate Literacy

Urban adult-literacy programs are as varied as the adult students they serve. Students may be immigrants and foreign-born professionals learning English as a Second Language, incarcerated adults pursuing their GEDs, parents wanting to help their children with homework, unemployed adults seeking job-related skills. Literacy centers are as tenuously funded and supported as the schools, community colleges, community centers, libraries, and other institutions they occupy.

My colleagues and I entered this textured but typical adult-literacy landscape representing a professional development-and-research arm of a large urban university. We were providing professional development to teachers from an urban alternative high school system undergoing reorganization. This professional development consisted of eight daylong workshops spread over the school year and monthly on-site visits and mentoring. In the course of planning and conducting workshops and school visits, we noted that mass media were intrinsic to the lives of the participants and could be tapped in various ways to foster literacy teaching and learning for both the literacy teachers and the literacy students. Our approach to providing professional development to the teachers was based on student-centered adult-learning principles, which recognize prior experience, different learning styles, and different levels of self-direction (Grow, 1991). We saw the adult learner as inseparable from her or his context and culture. We strived to create a learning environment that was safe and resource rich and that encouraged critical thinking (Brookfield, 1987). In working with teachers, we modeled respectful, multivoiced discussion in the hope that the teachers would identify with their students and their experiences as adult learners.

New Directions for Adult and Continuing Education • DOI: 10.1002/ace

Parallels could be made between the teachers' and students' situations. The learners in these alternative high schools often had not had successful experiences in school. They often came to class distrustful, not understanding the relevance of classwork to their out-of-school lives. Likewise, the literacy teachers' past experiences with professional development and support were often disappointing to these educators. We were aware of the tension teachers experienced as their school system changed and they were increasingly held accountable for test scores.

After a teacher confided that she was frustrated that she could not imbue her students with her excitement for mathematics, she and the professional developer devised a numeracy lesson in the format of the TV game show *Jeopardy*. After careful preparation, they introduced the activity. All the students were familiar with the program and knew that answers had to be given in the form of questions. Students worked in teams. The categories were place values, operations, graphs/definitions, and roman numerals, all challenging topics for these students. Where quiet and private the week before, the students became animated, engaged, and loud with the new format. They were comfortable voicing their disappointments and triumphs with loud moans and cheers. After one round, they clamored to create their own "answers." The teacher used this format not only for numeracy lessons but also for history and other subjects. One student said that he never watched *Jeopardy* (although he was familiar with its format) but now he would and would try to answer the questions. This experience suggests again how much TV is interwoven with people's lives and the value of recognizing these out-of-school habits. It also suggests how learners can gain confidence and a broadened outlook. The competition aspect may have appealed to these learners as well as the built-in pacing and opportunities for small victories.

As a second example, during one of the daylong workshops, the literacy teachers watched a video, *Who Moved My Cheese*. Although this video was specifically created for training and education purposes, the teachers were mesmerized with the cartoon version of the popular book about dealing with change, and they reacted strongly in animated discussions. But it seemed that most saw little immediate connection between this parable and their own situation. Later, however, many asked to see the video again and in subsequent journaling indicated further thinking about the message. In this case, they could more readily identify others' behavior than their own. Their experience speaks to the impact of the visual media; the message stayed with the teachers although they were passively, it seemed, watching a cartoon. Visual media, even those created specifically for educational purposes, connect to everyday media and literacy practices, and for that reason they are likely to have appeal. The teachers were able to move from a literal recounting of the steps involved in the process of change depicted in the cartoon to a deeper grasp of the change occurring in their school system and how they were dealing with it. These insights about themselves

New Directions for Adult and Continuing Education • DOI: 10.1002/ace

and their institutions were reassuring and transferable. The presentation of the sensitive topic in animated, up-beat form seemed to set the stage for constructive, problem-solving discussion.

As a third example, during another workshop literacy teachers used newspapers and popular magazines to create posters around topics like entrepreneurship, sight words, and careers. This low-tech activity took on a life of its own as the participants considered and critiqued ads, images, headlines, their implications, their sources, and their usefulness. They did not want the activity to end, in part because they were enjoying the familiar, comfortable medium, the tactile manipulation, and the social aspects of their small-group project. Unprompted, they questioned sources and evaluated messages. For example, they asked why a magazine image of a business meeting included only white males and considered the message this picture would send to their adult students if used in the classroom poster. Here was the potential for a discussion of how gender, race, and class are often portrayed in the media and a way to facilitate critical media literacy.

These three activities tapped into the media-usage habits of adult learners and not surprisingly showed their comfort and familiarity with television game shows, videos, and magazines. In using a well-known TV game, *Jeopardy,* our intent was not to duplicate the out-of-school experience, but as Mahiri (2004) suggests, to appreciate how engagement in popular culture "connects to students' personal identity, their needs to construct meanings and their pursuit of pleasures and personal power" (p. 382). We were using as models media formats adult learners explore routinely and are familiar with. They responded with intense involvement and demonstrated they were actively evaluating and reflecting on the content.

These three examples are replicated daily by adult educators who use mass media in innovative and critical ways. They show how mass media, in addition to providing entertainment, can serve as learning resources. Our examples, although not particularly detailed, show how one can draw on media-usage habits in teaching literacy as opposed to focusing on the development of critical media-literacy skills. They illustrate how inseparable popular media are from our lives and suggest the learning advantages of their formats, delivery, and content, especially for urban adults (Morrell, 2002).

Recommendations and Implications

Tapping into the popular media-usage habits of literacy teachers and students has several implications for practice. First, we can include popular media when we consider adult learners' backgrounds. We can ask about how they use television, radio, magazines, and newspapers for individual, informal learning. Their responses may indicate their different learning styles, different stages of self-directedness, motivations, and previous experience and can be used to inform a student-centered approach.

New Directions for Adult and Continuing Education • DOI: 10.1002/ace

Second, in understanding the informal media-use habits of the adult learner, we can not only delve into the needs that are being met by their use but also design bases for critical viewing, listening, and reading. Finding out how adult learners are habitually using these media, we can foster their personal critical media literacy. Problem posing and questioning content, delivery, origins, and intent, as well as looking at how different social groups are portrayed in the media, can lead to new perspectives and critical awareness.

Third, dialogue about the common experience of media use can also begin to foster a sense of community in the learning environment. For example, the literacy teachers and students were all familiar with *Jeopardy* and could engage further with this shared experience, as they also could undoubtedly do with other popular television shows, movies, or music. Further, learners not familiar with popular media because they are from a different culture or nation can be encouraged to share an aspect of popular media from their own culture or nation, and teachers can use such examples for the further development of literacy skills.

Fourth, different types of media can be manipulated in specific ways that can increase possibilities for dialogue and for the development of literacy in multiple forms. We can take advantage of the physical features of mass media for learning. Videos can be replayed, frames frozen, clips selected, so that learners can revisit them. Newspapers and magazines can be cut, pasted, and rearranged. These manipulations can address individual learning styles and preferences as well as opportunities to re-view something to examine it from multiple perspectives.

In conclusion, a social definition of what it means to be literate appreciates the process of situated meaning making. Popular media present comfortable, known frameworks that may meet individual needs for private learning and learning by observation. The highly visual aspects of most media correspond to many learning styles. The pace and competition aspects of television and video games make them engaging and exciting ways to learn (Gee, 2003). Appreciating that there are different yet effective ways to be literate in one's world and overcoming the "deficit" perspective of adult literacy may take time in the face of today's accountability and test-score mentality. But the recognition that adult learning is always contextualized and positionalized can lead us to further study the ways that adult non-readers learn from popular media. Building on adults' use of popular media validates their approaches, and using mass media brings them into a common conversation.

References

Bates, A. E. "Literacy by Radio: Lessons from Around the World." Paper presented at the International Symposium of Popular Literacy by Radio, Dominican Republic, 1990.

Beder, H., and Medina, P. "Classroom Dynamics in Adult Literacy Education." National Center for the Study of Adult Learning and Literacy (NCSALL) Report 18. Cambridge, Mass.: Harvard Graduate School of Education, 1999.

Brookfield, S. D. *Developing Critical Thinkers.* San Francisco: Jossey-Bass, 1987.

Buckingham, D., and Sefton-Green, J. *Cultural Studies Goes to School: Reading and Teaching Popular Media.* London: Taylor & Francis, 1994.

Centre for Literacy. "Adult Literacy and Television: Has a Familiar Tool Been Overlooked?" *Literacy Across the Curriculumedia Focus,* 2000, *15*(1), 16–18.

Donnelly, M. "An American Experiment TV411: Reaching Learners Out of Class—the Pilot Year Research." *Literacy Across the Curriculumedia Focus,* 2000, *15*(1), 27–29.

Fingeret, H. A. *It Belongs to Me: A Guide to Portfolio Assessment in Adult Education Programs.* Durham, N.C.: Literacy South, 1993. (ED 359 352)

Fingeret, H. A., and Drennon, C. *Literacy for Life: Adult Learners, New Practices.* New York: Teachers College, Columbia University, 1997.

Gee, J. P. *What Video Games Have to Teach Us About Learning and Literacy.* New York: St. Martin's Press, 2003.

Grow, G. "Teaching Learners to Be Self-Directed. A Stage Approach." *Adult Education Quarterly,* 1991, *41*(3), 125–149.

Holland, C. *Literacy and the New Word Order: An International Literature Review.* Leicaster, U.K.: National Institute of Adult Continuing Education, 1998.

Kaestle, C., and others. *Adult Literacy and Education in America.* NCES 2001-534. Washington, D.C.: National Center of Education Statistics, Office of Educational Research and Improvement, U.S. Department of Education, 2001.

Lewis, A. "Talking About Media Experiences: Everyday Life as Pop Culture." *Journal of Popular Culture,* 1982, *16*(3), 106.

Mahiri, J. (ed.). *What They Don't Learn in School: Literacy in the Lives of Urban Youth.* New York: Peter Lang, 2004.

Marsick, V., and Watkins, K. "Informal and Incidental Learning." In S. Merriam (ed.), *The New Update on Adult Learning Theory.* San Francisco: Jossey-Bass, 2001.

Merrifield, J., Bingman, M. B., Hemphill, D., and deMarais, K.P.B. *Life at the Margins: Literacy, Language and Technology in Everyday Life.* New York: Teachers College Press, 1997.

Morrell, E. "Toward a Critical Pedagogy of Popular Culture: Literacy Development Among Urban Youth." *Journal of Adolescent and Adult Literacy,* 2002, *46*(1), 72–77.

Quigley, B. A. *Rethinking Literacy Education: The Critical Need for Practice-Based Change.* San Francisco: Jossey-Bass, 1997.

Riesman, D. "Listening to Popular Music." *American Quarterly* (John Hopkins University), 1950, 359–371.

Singh, E. "Using Television/Video for Adult Learning." *Literacy Across the Curriculumedia Focus,* 2000, *15*(1), 16–18.

Street, B. V. *Literacy and Development: Ethnographic Perspectives in Theory and Practice.* New York: Routledge, 2001.

Tait, A. A. "Our Message Is Not on the Media." In G. T. Meiss and A. A. Tait (eds.), *Ethnic Media in America: Images, Audiences and Transforming Forces.* Dubuque, Iowa: Kendell/Hunt, 2004.

Taylor, M. C. "Informal Adult Learning and Everyday Literacy Practices." *Journal of Adolescent and Adult Literacy,* 2006, *49*(6), 500–509.

BARBARA P. HEUER is assistant professor in and the coordinator of the Master's Program in Adult Education and Human Resource Development at Fordham University in New York City.

7

This chapter discusses the long-term impact on British women of the popular 1960s television show The Avengers *and explores strategies for utilizing popular culture to facilitate learning in the classroom.*

The Avengers, Public Pedagogy, and the Development of British Women's Consciousness

Robin Redmon Wright

A friend of mine who once worked as a marketing analyst for MTV often quips that she was forced into early retirement at twenty-nine because "no one could work there after thirty." As I've discussed elsewhere (Wright, 2007), according to her, the prevailing idea was that no one who reached the age of thirty could possibly understand marketing to MTV's young viewers. Now an associate professor of advertising at a major university, she has no regrets about her career moves. But her story is indicative of one reason many educators dismiss popular culture, especially television, as a teaching tool. How can teachers use what they do not understand or appreciate or promote that which does not seem to value them? Besides, how can adult educators determine which programs, music, and trends are having an impact on their students? Furthermore, when students range in age from eighteen to eighty, how can educators facilitate meaningful discussions of popular culture in the classroom?

Difficulties abound. Educators have to question whether the learning that results is worth the effort. Because popular culture is often fleeting and transitory, can it have a lasting impact on students? Does it produce meaning-making or temporary imitation? And even if informal learning is taking place in front of the television, is it possible—or even desirable—to attempt to connect to that learning in the classroom?

x

WILEY InterScience®
DISCOVER SOMETHING GREAT

NEW DIRECTIONS FOR ADULT AND CONTINUING EDUCATION, no. 115, Fall 2007 © 2007 Wiley Periodicals, Inc.
Published online in Wiley InterScience (www.interscience.wiley.com) • DOI: 10.1002/ace.268

63

My research indicates that such learning is lasting and may, indeed, be worth the effort. As Henry Giroux and Roger Simon (1989) assert, "Critical educators need to retheorize the importance of popular culture as a central category for both understanding and developing a theory and practice of critical pedagogy" (p. 4). Sometimes learning from popular television can be powerful, especially when an individual is desirous of change.

This chapter explains how the show *The Avengers,* a popular British television program with an unusual female lead role, captured the imagination of women viewers in England from 1962 to 1964. After describing the show and then the research project investigating viewers' responses to it, this chapter explores the experience of watching television as a space of public/popular pedagogy. It concludes by offering some suggestions for classroom practice.

The Avengers: **More Than a Cult TV Classic**

During feminism's first wave, Virginia Woolf ([1931] 1980) wrote about traditional British gender roles: "[There was an angel in every house who] was intensely sympathetic. She was intensely charming. She was utterly unselfish. She excelled in the difficult arts of family life. She sacrificed herself daily. If there was chicken, she took the leg; if there was a draught, she sat in it—in short, she was so constituted that she never had a mind or wish of her own, but preferred to sympathize always with the mind and wishes of others" (p. 17). That angel made women doubt their abilities, made them weak and submissive. It made them succumb to drudgery and servitude instead of realizing their talents and abilities. Woolf says of her struggle for a career, "I did my best to kill her. . . . I acted in self defense" (p. 17). That "phantom" angel was created in part by popular culture.

A shift in popular culture was necessary to bar that phantom from more than a few dwellings. Three decades after Woolf battled the angel in her house to realize her ambition as a writer, Honor Blackman, in the role of Dr. Catherine Gale, left a trail of bruised, battered, banned, and broken angels in her wake as the female half of the crime-fighting duo called the Avengers. In 1962, before the advent of second-wave feminism in Britain, Cathy Gale regularly challenged the status quo—which her partner, bowler-hatted John Steed, played by Patrick Macnee, personified. In the series, he is old school tie; she is black leather. She helps Steed only when he appeals to her sense of justice and humanitarianism. She challenges his cavalier attitude toward human rights, biological warfare, nuclear arms, and individual liberty amidst their ongoing debate about social and political issues. Before Gale, female characters on television were objects of ridicule, victims of crime, or the angels in the house. But as one of her fans told me, "After Cathy Gale, nothing was the same."

When Blackman replaced one of the two male leads in the successful, though fledgling, series, several scripts had already been written for two men.

New Directions for Adult and Continuing Education • DOI: 10.1002/ace

Budget constraints meant no new scripts or extensive rewrites, so Blackman read and acted a part that had been written for a man. The result was the development of a female character with traits that were traditionally male: physical strength, decisiveness, intellectual superiority, tenacity, and independence. When the writers eventually began writing for Blackman, she was unhappy with the result. With the support of her co-star, Macnee, and the producer, Leonard White, she insisted that the writers "write it for a man. When I deliver it nobody will think it's male dialogue"(Soter, p. 75, 2001). She deliberately inverted the gendered nature of early 1960s cultural discourse by intentionally playing a role written for an actor with traditionally masculine traits and talents.

Gale developed as a character with a black belt in judo, a doctorate in anthropology, expertise with firearms, a history of humanitarianism, a past as both a freedom fighter and a big-game hunter, and a philosophy of humanism. She guest-lectured at erudite societies on a variety of topics, from her photographic trip down the Amazon to her anthropological research on remote African tribes. The producers wanted her to represent a cross between two unusual women, Margaret Mead and Margaret Bourke-White, the famous *Life* photographer (Miller, 1997; Rogers; 1989; Soter, 2000). She "transgressed gender definitions by displaying behavior normally reserved for males" (Andrae, 1996, p. 117)—shooting guns, wearing leather, riding motorcycles, throwing men across the room, and succeeding professionally.

White, the producer, insisted that the scripts eventually commissioned for John Steed and Cathy Gale, rather than the original duo, John Steed and David Keel, incorporate qualities rooted in Gale's personal ethics, activism, and humanistic convictions. In 1962, White cautioned the writers to connect Gale's involvement to her work: "Cathy <u>must</u> be correctly motivated. . . . She must have something <u>special</u> to contribute on the mission. So special that Steed <u>needs</u> her help. She must, above all, have the humanitarian and the moral attitude to the story. She wants to help those who are in peril or distress. She <u>cares</u> about them. This must of itself give rise to some <u>conflict</u> with STEED. His strictly professional and ruthless attitude will often enrage her" (quoted in Rogers, 1987, p. 15; italics and capitals in the original). Gale cared about people, even the criminals she helped catch. Although Gale worked to help people and might be seen as sympathetic, she bears no further resemblance to Woolf's "angel in the house." A typical exchange between the two leads provides an example: Steed drops by Gale's apartment and asks, "What's for breakfast?"; rather than demurely offering to cook, she counters with a sharp, "Cook it and see."

Women liked her. By 1964, both the character she portrayed and the actor herself had so much popular influence that the show was temporarily "banned in England for electoral interference" because the government feared that her appearance in a political commercial would unduly influence election results (Miller, 1997, p. 5). Blackman described Gale as "the first feminist to come to a television serial; the first woman to fight back" (quoted in Miller, 1997, p. 7); Gale was also hailed as "Britain's new symbol of womanhood" (Rogers, 1989, p. 15) and "the first feminist female lead" (Andrae, 1996, p. 115). Brian Clemens, writer of five Cathy Gale episodes and forty *Avengers* episodes with Steed's other partners, said in an interview with the author on August 24, 2006, "It was liberating for me, really, writing for Cathy Gale. I had to think about women in a new way."

The Power of a TV Character: Stories of Identity Development

For two years, I listened to stories told by Cathy Gale's contemporaneous women viewers. I have gathered documents about the show, including magazine and newspaper articles, videoed interviews, critical reviews, and audience statistics, for qualitative content analysis and background information. These artifacts, as well as interviews with some of the scriptwriters and Blackman herself, helped me set the context for the women's stories.

In *The Second Sex,* Simone de Beauvoir (1973), like Woolf, expresses frustration with women's limitations: "Woman is shut up in a kitchen or in a boudoir, and astonishment is expressed that her horizon is limited. Her wings are clipped and it is found deplorable that she cannot fly. Let but the future be opened to her, and she will no longer be compelled to linger in the present" (p. 605). For some of her women viewers, watching Gale opened the future by showing the future. According to Caren Deming (1990), "'Breaking the sequence', Woolf's term for rupturing the expected order of events in a narrative to break their hegemonic inevitability, is also possible in television" (p. 58). Gale, a character made androgynous to some extent by first being written for a male, ruptured the expected actions for female television characters. This break in the sequence of popular representations of women allowed viewers to see and, following Gale's example, to fight for a different future.

Several common threads emerged in the stories the women viewers recounted, but the most prevalent was the theme of defiance. They had grown up in postwar Britain, when women were encouraged to marry, stay home, and replenish the decimated population. Although women's work outside the home was valued, even demanded, during the war, Britain's government sought ways to send women home to have children in the late forties and early fifties. Parliament moved to "rebuild the family" with attention placed "squarely on the issue of 'adequate mothering' as the surest means to securing future social stability" (Lewis, 1992, p. 11). As one woman told me, "It wasn't just heresy to not want to marry and have babies, it was unpatriotic—almost criminal." Another agreed: "I grew up during the war [and] . . . it was all the same: one was expected to marry a soldier and have children." In a country/culture that once headed an empire that included almost a quarter of the known world, the pressure to conform was intense. Scriptwriter Jon Manchip White, whose work was intended for the original two male leads but was acted by Macnee and Blackman, confided that he never wrote good parts for women; they were always peripheral. He said he would not have written a part in which a woman physically fights a man. He "wouldn't have expected a woman, you know, to lash out and kick men in the whatsits" (interview with author, March 13, 2005). For him, women of that era always played supporting roles.

In that environment, Gale's female audience recognized that she had no problem kicking both men and traditional gender roles in the whatsits. They metaphorically followed suit. As one woman, now in her mid-sixties, expressed it, "I have always known that there is a genuine Cathy Gale element within my persona that is available . . . to help me to deal with difficult confrontational situations." Another woman took judo lessons in the 1970s and learned hand-to-hand combat. Smiling mischievously, she explained, "I never forgot Cathy's ability to fight men who were much bigger and stronger than she. It seemed so powerful, you know? I wanted to feel powerful, and I did." Watching the independent, intelligent, well-educated, and athletic Gale empowered some viewers by offering them an alternative to the women their culture told them to become.

One woman, now a scientist and researcher, compared Gale with other popular female characters, who "were pathetic women that fell over when the wind changed. . . . That was the other role model, pathetic creatures that needed help. . . . Women were not doing things. She [Gale] was the only one." One woman described several contemporaneous prime-time programs and the female roles in them: "They were meek, obedient wives and mothers who were sometimes brutalized by their husbands and sometimes just used by the men in the series, but none of them protested. It was accepted as inevitable. Their place. None stood up for herself. There was no one else like Cathy. They were all victims."

Several of the women spoke of Gale with an intimacy they might use when speaking of a longtime, close friend: "She helps me, Cathy does. When I feel nervous or apprehensive, I think to myself, 'What would Cathy do?'" One woman told me, chuckling: "I *am* her—Cathy Gale. I identify with her so strongly that I think I've become her. I walk like she walks and talk, I hope, as she talks." They have also quietly followed Blackman's career in theater and film as well as on television, speaking of her with a deep respect and appreciation and crediting her with changing the direction of their lives.

Most of the women also credit Blackman in her role as Gale for creating the look that changed London fashion forever. Cathy's head-to-toe leather outfits, worn for fight scenes, and her chic suits and hats, worn in scenes of her professional life, were a great influence on the fashion industry—but the effect didn't compare with the impact of her leather boots. Wearing boots with everything, Gale started a trend that has persisted as part of the fabric of London life. Blackman and co-star Macnee even released a recording called *Kinky Boots*. The recording punctuates the on-going impact. As one viewer emphatically stated, "To this day, when I have to deal with a difficult situation, I put on my boots thinking, 'I'll do as Cathy would do.'"

New Directions for Adult and Continuing Education • DOI: 10.1002/ace

All the women who contacted me for interviews are professionally successful, and they credited the example set by Gale for that success. Some told me they would not have gone to university were it not for Gale. One explained: "You'd do quite well if you learned to type and do shorthand and got an office job. But you were never expected to then be, one day, the boss. I mean, if you were really, really good and clever and you wanted a career, you'd be somebody's secretary." Watching Gale made her dream of other possibilities. Another woman cited Cathy's influence on her choice of a career in science. After all, Cathy had a Ph.D. and conducted research; why shouldn't she? She confided that her teachers told her, "Girls don't do science." But she always knew she could be a scientist. Another woman is a professional consultant who conducts workshops for women on female empowerment. She laughed as she told me, "I give seminars all over the world on how to act like Cathy Gale. I just call it something else." All of them still look to Gale as an example, a role model, and a mentor. I was fascinated as they revealed the depths of the impact that a TV character had on the formation of their identities as professional, feminist, empowered women. She is a role model they cling to still—with a vengeance.

Gale's viewers killed the angel in their houses and refused to allow their wings to be clipped, all because they had watched a woman in a prime-time crime drama show them what was possible. And they have continued to follow her example for over forty years.

Television and Pedagogy

Television has a strong influence on our students, irrespective of their age, and educators must recognize that its impact is significant. Stephen Brookfield (1986) emphasizes this point: "The 'effects' of television cannot be separated from their context and treated as isolated phenomena to which we are given limited exposure. On the contrary, television's influence is all-pervasive. . . . It shapes the framework of our political discourse" (p. 152). As my research indicates, television can be a powerful influence in the lives of women. Elisabeth Hayes (2000) notes, "Women's learning takes place in a wide variety of social contexts" (p. 23). One context is television, which, Paul Armstrong (2000) asserts, is "far from being about passive non-learning." He believes that "television viewing can have tremendous potential for stimulating critical commentary and raising awareness of a wide range of issues, not the least through popular cultural programs including soaps" (p. 2).

Educators of adults should help learners make sense of their experiences by connecting to the learning that takes place outside the classroom. Paulo Freire and Henry Giroux (1989) argue succinctly for this connection as they insist that pedagogy "must incorporate aspects of popular culture as a serious educational discourse" (p. ix). Giroux (1999) later argues that "public pedagogy" is performed through popular culture. He points out that media culture "has become a substantial, if not primary, educational force in regulating the meanings, values, and tastes that set the norms that offer up and legitimate particular subject positions—what it means to claim an identity as a male, female, white, black, citizen, noncitizen" (pp. 2–3).

David Gauntlett (2002) further claims that understanding the power of popular media is crucial for expanding gender awareness: "To destabilize the taken-for-granted assumptions about the supposedly binary divide between female and male, masculinity and femininity, gay and straight, what could be more powerful than a two-pronged attack, on the levels of both everyday life and popular media?" (p. 143). As educators, if we are to help students resist the pervasive binary thinking about gender or, in fact, most social, ethical, and political issues, popular media should be one of the first tools we employ.

The women in my study, like our students, formed their identities, in part, through television. According to Elizabeth Ellsworth (2005, p. 4), "The visual experience of watching a film . . . has a material nature that involves biological and molecular events taking place in the body of the viewer and in the physical and imagined space between the viewer and the film." Ellsworth believes that viewer responses to the experience of intensely engaging with a character or story is a "pedagogical anomaly" that is "difficult to see as *pedagogy* only when we view it from the 'center' of the dominant educational discourses and practices" (p. 5). But when we reject the view that "knowledge is a thing already made and learning is an experience already known," we can see the space between viewer and screen as "the experience of a learning self in the making and the term 'pedagog' can then be applied" (p. 5). This public pedagogy takes place in the body of the viewer and in the space between viewer and television. Educators can tap into that personal pedagogy to foster intellectual development and professional growth.

Adults experience television as a portal of learning about self/subject that contributes to their identity formation. Educators should view popular culture in adult lives and ask, "How do we use what has already been thought [of] as a provocation and call to invention?" (Ellsworth, 2005, p. 165). Part of our challenge as educators of adults is to foster critical awareness, identity development, and social change using the informal learning taking place in the spaces between our students and our media culture.

Suggestions for Practice

In order to use popular television to promote critical awareness and identity development or to use it as a vehicle for any educational objective, educators must make a concerted effort to know which programs their students are watching. On the first day of my classes, students complete a questionnaire that asks about their favorite hobbies, television shows, musical artists, movies, books, as well as about practical concerns such as hours worked per week and educational goals. I then incorporate aspects of the television, music, and films they enjoy most into the course objectives. Setting up such a flexible syllabus requires time-consuming work on my part, but, I am convinced, it elicits powerful and engaged prose, as well as the development of critical thinking. As a writing teacher, I am fortunate to be able to use discussions of popular culture to foster critical analysis, sociopolitical awareness, and improved academic writing.

Educators in all disciplines can benefit from incorporating popular culture into their teaching. Popular television has often been used in adult-literacy programs. However, in his discussion of adult learning via television, Armstrong asserts that "television is more than a vehicle for developing literacy. From a liberatory perspective, television has its own literacy that needs to be critically decoded and interpreted" (2000, p. 4). In addition, teachers of developmental reading and writing courses can draw from students' engagement with television to develop awareness of and foster active engagement with new ideas. Doing so not only helps develop reading and writing skills and techniques but also prepares students for the critical thinking required for college-level work and active citizenship.

Educators in a variety of disciplines have begun to explore the value of using popular media to facilitate student learning. For example, the National Council of Teachers of Mathematics has developed a Web site to help teachers teach math using the popular television crime drama *NUMB3RS* ("Teachers and Students," 2006). Karen Anijar (2000) uses critical analysis of *Star Trek* as a basis for thinking about current social and political issues. Adult educators would do well to make use of these and other resources.

Conclusion

In his discussion of Michel Foucault's "technologies of the self" and media, Gauntlett (2002) suggests that "an individual's ethics are manifested in their mindset and actions." He further argues that "'technologies of the self' refers to the ways in which people put forward, and police their 'selves' in society; and the ways in which available discourses may enable or discourage various practices of self" (p. 125). Popular television is an available discourse that educators cannot ignore. It is powerful and, as Brookfield points out, all-pervasive, and it is often much more accessible to our students than is academic discourse. Popular culture thus helps develop the ethics, the practices of self, the identities, and the moral foundations of our students. As the results of *The Avengers* study indicate, it is often instrumental in forming our gender consciousness and adult identities. As adult educators, we must pay attention to the powerful influence of the popular.

My friend who left MTV at the age of twenty-nine is still one of the hippest people I know. Her university students benefit from her insatiable curiosity about what is currently "in." Like my friend, we should make an effort, even though we may be past age twenty-nine, to connect with the MTV/iPod generation. Many adult learners are making connections between the classroom and popular culture with or without our facilitation. It is imperative that we identify the parts of popular culture that interest and entertain our students. In setting an example of lifelong learning by being engaged with the popular media that our students value, we prove by our breadth of knowledge that educators of adults do, indeed, know about the world our students inhabit and that we can connect to it—no matter what our age.

References

Andrae, T. "Television's First Feminist: *The Avengers* and Female Spectatorship." *Discourse: Berkeley Journal for Theoretical Studies in Media and Culture,* 1996, *18*(3), 112–136.

Anijar, K. *Teaching Toward the 24th Century: Star Trek as Social Curriculum.* Bristol, Pa.: Falmer Press, 2000.

Armstrong, P. "All Things Bold and Beautiful: Researching Adult Learning Through Soaps." In V. L. Chapman (ed.), *Proceedings of the 41st Adult Education Research Conference.* Vancouver: University of British Columbia, 2000. Retrieved Feb. 2, 2002, from http://www.edst.educ.ubc.ca/aerc/2000/armstrongp1-web.htm.

Beauvoir, S. de. *The Second Sex.* (H. M. Parshley, trans.). New York: Vintage Press, 1973.

Brookfield, S. D. "Media Power and the Development of Media Literacy: An Adult Educational Interpretation." *Harvard Educational Review,* 1986, *56*(2), 151–170.

Deming, C. J. "For Television-Centered Television Criticism: Lessons from Feminism." In M. E. Brown (ed.), *Television and Women's Culture: The Politics of the Popular.* Thousand Oaks, Calif.: Sage, 1990.

Ellsworth, E. *Places of Learning: Media, Architecture, and Pedagogy.* New York: Routledge, 2005.

Freire, P., and Giroux, H. A. "Pedagogy, Popular Culture, and Public Life: An Introduction." In P. Freire and H. A. Giroux (eds.), *Popular Culture, Schooling, and Everyday Life.* New York: Bergin & Garvey, 1989.

Gauntlett, D. *Media, Gender, and Identity: An Introduction.* New York: Routledge, 2002.

Giroux, H. A. *The Mouse That Roared: Disney and the End of Innocence.* Lanham, Md.: Rowman & Littlefield, 1999.

Giroux, H. A., and Simon, R. "A Pedagogy of Pleasure and Meaning." In P. Freire & H. A. Giroux (eds.), *Popular Culture, Schooling, and Everyday Life.* New York: Bergin & Garvey, 1989.

Hayes, E. "Social Contexts." In E. Hayes and D. Flannery (eds.), *Women as Learners: The Significance of Gender in Adult Learning.* San Francisco: Jossey-Bass, 2000.

Lewis, J. *Women in Britain Since 1945: Women, Family, Work and the State in Post-War Years.* Oxford, U.K.: Blackwell, 1992.

Miller, T. *The Avengers.* London: British Film Institute, 1997.

Rogers, D. "A New Direction: Enter Cathy Gale." *Stay Tuned: The Officially Authorized Avengers Magazine,* 1987, *1*(2), 8–20.

Rogers, D. *The Complete Avengers: Everything You Ever Wanted to Know About* The Avengers *and* The New Avengers. New York: St. Martin's Press, 1989.

Soter, T. *Investigating Couples: A Critical Analysis of* The Thin Man, The Avengers, *and* The X-Files. Jefferson, N.C.: McFarland, 2000.

"Teachers and Students Give NUMB3RS a Thumbs Up." *NCTM New Bulletin,* May/June 2006, *42*(9), 1.

Woolf, V. "Professions for Women: A Paper Read to the Women's Service League in 1931." In M. Barrett (ed.), *Women and Writing*. Orlando: Harcourt Brace, 1980.

Wright, R. R. "Adult Education, Popular Culture, and Women's Identity Development: Self-Directed Learning with *The Avengers*." Unpublished doctoral dissertation. Department of Educational Administration and Human Resource Development, Texas A&M University, 2007.

ROBIN REDMON WRIGHT is assistant professor of college teaching and adult education at the University of Texas, San Antonio.

This chapter examines popular culture as a site of cultural resistance. Specifically, it explores how "culture jamming," a cultural-resistance activity, can be a form of adult education.

8

Popular Culture, Cultural Resistance, and Anticonsumption Activism: An Exploration of Culture Jamming as Critical Adult Education

Jennifer A. Sandlin

Since the mid-1990s, adult educators have become increasingly interested in consumption and consumerism and how they relate to adult learning and adult education. For instance, Robin Usher, Ian Bryant, and Rennie Johnston (1997) have urged adult educators to start taking consumption seriously; they point out that we are all "affected by consumer culture and consumerist discourse and images" (p. 15). Kaela Jubas (2006) has investigated what it means to be a "critical consumer-citizen" (p. 200) through an exploration of how the process of shopping socializes adults to be consumers while at the same time offering possibilities to resist consumerism and to learn about democratic citizenship. And I (Sandlin, 2004, 2005a) have explored how consumer education can been seen as a political site where learners can craft particular points of view on and relationships with consumer culture. Although educators of adults are starting to explore issues of consumption, much work remains to be done.

Adult educators also have become increasingly interested in popular culture as a site of informal learning. Paul Armstrong (2000, 2005), Stephen Brookfield (1986), Elizabeth Tisdell and Patricia Thompson (2006), Robin Wright (2006), Peter Jarvis (2005), and myself (Sandlin, 2005b) view the mass media in general, and specific forms of mass media such as soap

NEW DIRECTIONS FOR ADULT AND CONTINUING EDUCATION, no. 115, Fall 2007 © 2007 Wiley Periodicals, Inc.
Published online in Wiley InterScience (www.interscience.wiley.com) • DOI: 10.1002/ace.269

73

operas, television, and popular magazines, as forms of public education. These realms of informal adult education are often neglected by adult educators although they are widespread and gaining in popularity. Armstrong (2000) argues that adult educators must learn to "recognize and value a wide range of informal learning" (p. 16), including the learning centered on the products of popular culture.

In this chapter I examine adult education and learning as it intersects with both consumerism and popular culture. I focus on a growing social movement of individuals who are concerned about consumerism and who are confronting consumption through cultural resistance in and through popular culture. I concentrate specifically on how these anticonsumption social movements are practicing critical adult education in largely informal realms of learning, through a cultural-resistance strategy called *culture jamming*. I use as examples two such groups, *Adbusters* magazine and Reverend Billy and the Church of Stop Shopping, exploring them as critical sites of adult education and learning. I also discuss culture jamming as a form of popular pedagogy, as described by Henry Giroux (2004) and Elizabeth Ellsworth (2005).

Popular Culture, Cultural Resistance, and Public Pedagogy

John Storey (2006) argues that there are many definitions of *popular culture,* including culture that is well liked by many people, "inferior culture" (p. 5) (or what is left over after we cull out "high culture"), commercial culture produced for mass consumption, folk culture emanating from "authentic" working-class people, and a political site of struggle between dominant and subordinate social groups. This last definition most accurately captures the way I view popular culture. I draw heavily from the view of popular culture that is grounded in a Gramscian cultural-studies framework. In this view, popular culture does not consist simply of cultural commodities such as film, television shows, and magazines (Storey, 1999, 2006). Rather, these commodities are the raw materials, provided by the culture industries, that people use to create popular culture. Storey (2006) states, "We need to see ourselves—all people, not just vanguard intellectuals—as active participants in culture: selecting, rejecting, making meanings, attributing value, resisting and, yes, being duped and manipulated" (p. 171). This perspective on popular culture thus conceptualizes it as an active, rather than a passive, process.

Also contained within a Gramscian view is the idea that what is important about popular culture is not its aesthetics but its politics—that is, its intersection with power (Bennett, 1998). Thus, popular culture is a site of conflict, where individuals resist, negotiate, and accommodate power relations. Stephen Duncombe (2002) explains this idea:

> Both the culture we enjoy and the culture in which we live provide us with
> ideas of how things are and how they should be, frameworks through which to

interpret reality and possibility. They help us account for the past, make sense of the present and dream of the future. Culture can be, and is, used as a means of social control. More effective than any army is a shared conception that the way things are is the way things should be. The powers-that-be don't remain in power by convincing us that they are the answer, but rather that there is no other solution. But culture can be, and is, used as a means of resistance, a place to formulate other solutions. In order to strive for change, you have first to imagine it, and culture is the repository of imagination (p. 35).

In other words, popular culture is always at once a site of hegemonic power and of political resistance.

Much has been written about how popular culture works to inculcate dominant values in individuals (Giroux, 1999). Therefore, instead of focusing on how popular culture reproduces inequalities, I describe here how it works as a means of resistance. *Resistance* consists of acts of opposition to dominant culture that contain within them a critique of domination and a struggle for self and social emancipation (Giroux, 2001). Resistance celebrates the power of human agency and stresses the fact that individuals are not simply passive victims of social structures. Resistance theories explore how people struggle with societal structures and create their own meanings through these negotiations (Solorzano and Delgado Bernal, 2001). In short, they focus on the power of human agency to question, reject, modify, or incorporate dominant ideologies and cultures; to critique oppression; and to work toward social justice (Giroux, 2001).

Cultural resistance is defined by Duncombe (2002) as "culture that is used, consciously or unconsciously, effectively or not, to resist and/or change the dominant political, economic and/or social structure" (p. 5). Raymond Williams (1973) states that through cultural resistance people can create and maintain ideas that oppose those of the dominant society. Examples of cultural resistance—or using popular culture to resist—include the activities of subcultures such as the mods, rude boys, teddy boys, and skinheads of 1960s Britain, as described by Dick Hebdige (1979); more recent subcultures including punk "straightedgers" and "ravers," or youth who are part of rave scenes; various forms of alternative and counter-hegemonic music from hip hop to Riot Grrrl bands; and 'zines and other DIY (do-it-yourself) magazines. Duncombe (2002) explains that individuals and groups practicing cultural resistance actively engage in creating popular culture, crossing the line "from consumer to creator" (p. 4). He also argues that cultural resistance provides a free space for creating new ideas to resist the dominant culture, helps build community, and can provide entrée into political resistance and can itself become political resistance. In exploring cultural resistance, Duncombe (2002) also urges us to pay attention to its educational process—that is, to focus on how politics is conveyed through popular culture—through examining the roles played by cultural content, form, and interpretation and the activity of cultural creation.

New Directions for Adult and Continuing Education • DOI: 10.1002/ace

These views of popular culture and resistance are echoed by educational scholars who focus on popular culture as a site of learning. *Public pedagogy* refers to the education provided by popular culture; popular culture teaches audiences and participants through the ways it represents people and issues and the kinds of discourses it creates and disseminates. Culture is where "identities are continually being transformed and power enacted" (Giroux, 2000, p. 354). Ellsworth's (2005) current perspectives on public pedagogy are especially helpful in exploring how culture jamming works in adult education. Ellsworth urges educators to pay attention to informal sites of learning such as public art installations and museums—what she calls "anomalous places of learning"—and to focus on their "pedagogical hinges"—the aspects that make them powerful sites of learning and teaching (p. 5). I borrow from Ellsworth a way of thinking of education within popular culture as an ongoing, active, creative process. To Ellsworth, public pedagogy works best when it creates transitional spaces—that is, when it helps us connect our inner realities to people, objects, and places outside ourselves.

Culture Jamming as Critical Public Pedagogy

I am currently in the process of collecting and analyzing data for a study of culture jamming as a site of adult learning. In this chapter I share some initial insights that begin to reveal how culture jamming works. I focus specifically on two culture-jamming groups, Adbusters Media Foundation and Reverend Billy and the Church of Stop Shopping. *Adbusters* is a magazine produced by the Adbusters Media Foundation, based in Vancouver. The magazine has two main themes—the ways in which marketing and mass media colonize space and the ways in which global capitalism and rampant consumption are destroying natural environments (Rumbo, 2002). A reader-supported, not-for-profit magazine with an international circulation of eighty-five thousand, *Adbusters* contains reader-supplied letters and articles, commentaries by activists from around the world, and photographs and stories highlighting readers' social dissent. *Adbusters* also hosts a Web site (www.adbusters.org) where activists can read about anticonsumption campaigns; download activist resources and flyers for distribution; and post and read information about their own and others' activism.

Bill Talen, whose stage character is Reverend Billy, is a political-theater artist who adopts the persona of a Southern evangelical preacher. Reverend Billy, leader of the Church of Stop Shopping, stages "retail interventions" and political performances in public spaces and retail stores along with the Stop Shopping Gospel Choir. He also writes "intervention manuals" such as the "Starbucks Invasion Kit" and other scripts that activists can use in their own public-theater jams. He stages "comic theatrical service[s]" (Lane, 2002, p. 60), structured as comic church services, with "readings from the saints (or the devils), public confessions, collective exorcisms, the honoring of new saints, donations to the cause, a lively choir, and a rousing sermon"

New Directions for Adult and Continuing Education • DOI: 10.1002/ace

(Lane, 2002, p. 61). During these services he performs a call-and-response style of preaching as the audience responds with "Hallelujah!" and "Amen!"

Culture jamming has been called an "insurgent political movement" (Harold, 2004, p. 190) that works against "the advertising-saturated, corporate-ruled consumer culture" (Bordwell, 2002, p. 237). The phrase *culture jamming* was coined in 1984 by the San Francisco–based electronica band Negitivland in reference to the illegal interruption of ham-radio signals (Carducci, 2006), but many culture jammers see themselves as descendents of the Situationists, a 1950s European anarchist group led by Guy Debord (Harold, 2004). Members of this group were concerned with fighting the "spectacle" of everyday life—""modern society's 'spectacular' level of commodity consumption and hype" (Lasn, 1999, p. 100). The spectacle stifles spontaneity, free will, and active living and replaces them with prepackaged experiences (Lasn, 1999). Culture jammers, like the Situationists before them, reject the passive consumption of consumer culture and seek to be active creators who live authentically.

1. Culture jamming takes many forms; it includes such cultural activities as producing and disseminating "subvertisements," hosting and participating in virtual protests using the internet, enacting "placejamming" projects (in which public spaces are reclaimed), and participating in DIY (do it yourself)political theater and "shopping interventions." Culture jamming "seeks to undermine the marketing rhetoric of multinational corporations, specifically through [such] practices as media hoaxing, corporate sabotage, billboard 'liberation,' and trademark infringement" (Harold, 2004, p. 190). I see these various modes of culture jamming as constituting "anomalous pedagogies." I believe the educational power of culture jamming lies in its ability to open "transitional spaces" through creativity and cultural production, create community, engage with the learner and the "teacher" corporeally, and provide entrée into and enact politics. I further locate culture jamming's pedagogical hinge in the ways it creates possibilities for change in audience members.

Opening Transitional Spaces Through Cultural Production. As a form of cultural resistance, culture jamming is a free space where artists and activists can "experiment with new ways of seeing and being" and where they can "develop tools and resources for resistance" (Duncombe, 2002, p. 5). *Adbusters*, for instance, encourages submissions from readers; most of the content of the magazine is created and contributed by readers. Reverend Billy invites audience participation during his "revivals"; through his Web site (www.revbilly.com) audience members can discuss issues such as consumerism and strategies for creating awareness among ordinary consumers. Reverend Billy's Web site hosts scripts of performance pieces that audience members can take, change, and enact in their local contexts. Reverend Billy also encourages his audiences to create and enact their own performance art. Culture jammers are redefining what it means to "read" a magazine and to enter into a "shopping experience."

New Directions for Adult and Continuing Education • DOI: 10.1002/ace

Culture jammers thus alter the ways in which public space and popular-culture commodities and experiences are created and used. Culture jammers create *transitional spaces,* which are spaces of play, creativity, and cultural production; transitional spaces help us bridge the boundaries between the self and the other. When we are in those spaces, "we are entertaining strangeness and playing in difference. We are crossing that important internal boundary that is the line between the person we have been but no longer are and the person we will become" (Ellsworth, 2005, p. 62). Culture jammers turn typically passive activities into active ones. In doing so they are creating culture rather than simply absorbing it. They redefine themselves and their relationships with consumption; they redefine possibilities for the future. As one reader/contributor to *Adbusters* wrote, "Another world is possible" ("Another World," 2003, p. 50).

Creating Community. As culture is created by culture jammers, it is also shared among them. Duncombe (2002) states that popular culture thus "becomes a focal point around which to build a community" (p. 6). Ellsworth (2005) argues that an important part of the education for democracy that takes place in public spaces is that it puts us in relation to each other "in ways we have never been before" (p. 95). I believe that both the act of creating culture together and the sharing of that culture help culture jammers and their audiences create community. Participating in culture jamming—for instance, in "liberating" billboards by changing the content of their messages—creates a powerful community for those doing the jamming. Culture jammers also offer audience members ways of relating to each other that they have never experienced before.

Engaging the Body and the Emotions. According to Ellsworth (2005), effective pedagogy must engage the entire learner. Part of the power of culture jamming as adult education lies in its ability to engage both the body and the emotions in a process of "becoming." First, the act of culture jamming often literally involves the body. For instance, one of Reverend Billy's "retail interventions," posted on his Web site, is a culture-jamming activity targeted at Starbucks. During this intervention, entitled "It's a Party! Bump and Grind the Buckheads," jammers filling a Starbucks store proceed to dance, strip, and hand out pamphlets. Reverend Billy explains the physical sensations that culture jamming ignites when he tries to reach his audience with his anticonsumption message. Audience members have to "embody the fun [of not consuming]. It all comes down to the decision, what sort of dance am I involved in here? Where are my arms, where are my hands? How far is my voice reaching, what am I saying? It's all physical. It's the physical-spiritual" (Reverend Billy, quoted in Ashlock, 2005). Second, culture jammers engage both their own and their audiences' emotions as they conduct their jams. For instance, one audience member explained his emotional reaction to one of Reverend Billy's public appearances, stating how suddenly feeling alive stirred up a sense of hope that is leading him to reconceptualize his identity.

New Directions for Adult and Continuing Education • DOI: 10.1002/ace

Enacting Politics. Cultural resistance can provide an entrée into political resistance and can itself become political resistance (Duncombe, 2002). In fact, part of culture jamming's effectiveness as pedagogy is its ability to help participants engage in politics. When political resistance is presented or enacted through culture—and especially through a fun, exciting experience of culture—it can seem more friendly and perhaps less threatening than other forms of political protest. Duncombe (2002) argues that "because cultural resistance often speaks in a more familiar and less demanding voice than political dissent it makes this move . . . easier. In this way cultural resistance works as a sort of stepping stone into political activity" (p. 6).

Culture jamming itself can also be considered political resistance, as it plays with and challenges dominant ways of doing, seeing, and experiencing culture. Duncombe (2002) argues that politics is essentially a cultural discourse—"a shared set of symbols and meanings that we all abide by" (p. 6). The politics of culture is conveyed through its content, form, interpretation, and the activity of production (Duncombe, 2002). Thus when culture jammers alter that discourse, shake it up, and envision new, more democratic discourses—change the content, the form, the ways it is interpreted, and the activities of its production—they are, in fact, enacting political resistance.

Culture Jamming's Pedagogical Hinge. All the pedagogical capacities thus far discussed involve leading learners to a moment of *détournement* (a turning around), in which they are no longer who they used to be but are caught off guard with the possibility of becoming someone different. I thus believe that the pedagogical hinge of culture jamming—an important learning moment—occurs when audience members experience détournement. *Adbusters* founder Kalle Lasn (1999) argues that culture jamming helps provide a new way of looking at the world; Lasn describes détournement as "a perspective-jarring turnabout in your everyday life" (p. xvii). He believes that détournement helps provide people with new choices about how to live and how to be: "You are—everyone is—a creator of situations, a performance artist, and the performance, of course, is your life, lived in your own way. . . . Many times a day, each of us comes to a little fork in the path. We can then do one of two things: act the way we normally, reflexively act, or do something a little risky and wild, but genuine. We can choose to live our life as 'a moral, poetic, erotic, and almost spiritual refusal' [Plant, 1992, p. 8] to cooperate with the demands of consumer culture" (p. 101).

Activists, through their culture jamming, are seeking to ignite détournement, to incite authenticity. As one culture jammer writing in *Adbusters* stated, "Is your life a project? Do you give a shit about anything? Can you still get angry? Be spontaneous?" ("Is Your Life a Project?" 2005). Détournement thus works as a form of transitional space in that it "opens up the space and time between an experience and our habitual response to it. It gives us time and space to come up with some other way of being in relation at that moment. It introduces a stutter, a hesitation. It jams the binary logics that keep self/other, inner/outer, individual/social locked in face-to-face opposition. It is a space where the skin-to-skin face-off between self and other has been pried apart so that a reordering of self and other can be set in motion and so that we might go on relating to each other at all" (Ellsworth, 2005, p. 64).

Conclusion

Nadine Dolby (2003), writing primarily for the K–12 educational realm, argues that educators who are concerned with democracy must extend their conception of teaching and learning "well beyond the schoolhouse" (p. 276). As educators of adults, we have long recognized the importance of the learning and education that goes on outside formal institutions. However, we are still largely ignoring the public pedagogy of popular culture, including the many ways in which adult learners are using cultural resistance to create democratic and empowering forms of popular culture and public spaces. We need to recognize the important learning that is happening outside formal adult education spaces in the realms of popular culture. The culture jammers I have described in this chapter are providing adult education, specifically with regard to the politics of consumption. These examples can be useful to adult educators, especially those interested in social justice.

First, they show how adults as learners are shaped by and actively re-create popular culture. Culture jammers "talk back" to and through popular culture—they name and make problematical the kinds of social relations and ideologies constructed through popular-culture commodities and experiences. They illustrate how we can view such commodities and experiences not as a fixed text that learners consume but as ongoing events or experiences (Giroux and Simon, 1989). These culture jammers also show how adult learners remake and appropriate the meanings of popular-culture commodities and experiences. As adult educators, we need to recognize this important aspect of identity formation and learning; we must include learners' engagement with popular culture when we draw on and build on their experiences, a hallmark of adult education practice. Paraphrasing Giroux and Simon (1989), we need to ask whether learners are able to see a connection between what we do in class and the lives they live outside of class, and we must devise ways to bring aspects of learners' lived culture into our classrooms.

Second, because critical adult education should be about the construction and production of knowledge, not just the consumption of it, the culture-jamming groups highlighted in this chapter can act as examples of classroom "prefigurative communities" (Epstein, 2002, p. 333). Social activist groups often try to structure their organizations and activities to be models for, or to prefigure, the kind of ideal society they are striving to create. Culture jammers participate in the creation of culture and knowledge, enact politics, open transitional spaces, create community,

New Directions for Adult and Continuing Education • DOI: 10.1002/ace

and engage their whole selves—intellect, body, and emotions. Culture jamming as pedagogy is an active "doing" rather than a passive "theorizing" (Hartley, 2002, p. 54). Culture jammers see culture as an active, two-way process; they refuse to be passive recipients of corporate-produced culture and instead produce their own (Hartley, 2002). In critical adult education classrooms, learners should be creating their own knowledges and cultures—becoming cultural producers, building new, more democratic cultural realities and spheres (Giroux, 2004). This depiction of culture jamming as education thus embodies what critical adult education could look like.

References

"Another World." *Adbusters #49,* 2003, *11*(5), 50.

Armstrong, P. "All Things Bold and Beautiful: Researching Adult Learning Through Soaps." In T. J. Sork, V. Chapman, and R. St. Clair (eds.), *Proceedings of the 41st Annual Adult Education Research Conference.* Vancouver: University of British Columbia, 2000.

Armstrong, P. "*The Simpsons* and Democracy: Political Apathy, Popular Culture, and Lifelong Learning as Satire." In R. Hill and R. Kiely (eds.), *Proceedings of the 46th Annual Adult Education Research Conference.* Athens: University of Georgia, 2005.

Ashlock, J. "Shopocalypse Now!: Q+A with Reverend Billy." *RES Magazine,* 2005, 8. Retrieved Jan. 5, 2007, from http://www.res.com/magazine/articles/shopocalypsenowqawithreverendbilly_2005-05-19.html.

Bennett, T. *Culture: A Reformer's Science.* Thousand Oaks, Calif.: Sage, 1998.

Bordwell, M. "Jamming Culture: Adbusters' Hip Media Campaign Against Consumerism." In T. Princen, M. Maniates, and K. Conca (eds.), *Confronting Consumption.* Cambridge, Mass.: MIT Press, 2002.

Brookfield, S. D. "Media Power and the Development of Media Literacy: An Adult Educational Interpretation." *Harvard Educational Review,* 1986, *56*(2), 151–170.

Carducci, V. "Culture Jamming: A Sociological Perspective." *Journal of Consumer Culture,* 2006, *6*(1), 116–138.

Dolby, N. "Popular Culture and Democratic Practice." *Harvard Educational Review,* 2003, *73*(3), 258–284.

Duncombe, S. *Cultural Resistance Reader.* New York: Verso, 2002.

Ellsworth, E. *Places of Learning: Media, Architecture, and Pedagogy.* New York: Routledge, 2005.

Epstein, B. "The Politics of Prefigurative Community." In S. Duncombe (ed.), *Cultural Resistance Reader.* New York: Verso, 2002.

Giroux, H., and Simon, R. I. (Eds.) *Popular Culture, Schooling, and Everyday Life.* New York: Bergin & Garvey, 1989.

Giroux, H. A. *The Mouse That Roared: Disney and the End of Innocence.* Lanham, Md.: Rowman & Littlefield, 1999.

Giroux, H. A. "Public Pedagogy as Cultural Politics: Stuart Hall and the 'Crisis' of Culture." *Cultural Studies,* 2000, *14*(2), 341–360.

Giroux, H. A. *Theory and Resistance in Education: Towards a Pedagogy for the Opposition.* New York: Bergin & Garvey, 2001.

Giroux, H. A. "Cultural Studies, Public Pedagogy, and the Responsibility of Intellectuals." *Communication and Critical/Cultural Studies,* 2004, *1*(1), 59–79.

Harold, C. "Pranking Rhetoric: 'Culture Jamming' as Media Activism." *Critical Studies in Media Communication,* 2004, *21*(3), 189–211.

Hartley, J. *Communication, Cultural and Media Studies: The Key Concepts.* New York: Routledge, 2002.

Hebdige, D. *Subculture: The Meaning of Style.* London: Methuen, 1979.

"Is Your Life a Project?" *Adbusters #49,* 2005, *11*(5), 88–89.

Jarvis, C. "Real Stakeholder Education? Lifelong Learning in the Buffyverse." *Studies in the Education of Adults,* 2005, *37*(1), 31–46.

Jubas, K. "The Trouble with Shopping: Discourses, Practices and Pedagogies of the Consumer-Citizen." In M. Hagen and E. Goff (eds.), *Proceedings of the 47th Annual Adult Education Research Conference.* Minneapolis: University of Minnesota, 2006.

Lane, J. "Reverend Billy: Preaching, Protest, and Postindustrial Flânerie." *Drama Review,* 2002, *46*(1), 60–84.

Lasn, K. *Culture Jam: How to Reverse America's Suicidal Consumer Binge—and Why We Must.* New York: HarperCollins, 1999.

Plant, S. *The Most Radical Gesture.* New York: Routledge, 1992.

Rumbo, J. D. "Consumer Resistance in a World of Advertising Clutter: The Case of *Adbusters.*" *Psychology & Marketing,* 2002, *19*(2), 127–148.

Sandlin, J. A. "Consumerism, Consumption, and a Critical Consumer Education for Adults." In R. St. Clair and J. A. Sandlin (eds.), *Promoting Critical Practice in Adult Education.* New Directions for Adult and Continuing Education, no. 102. San Francisco: Jossey-Bass, 2004.

Sandlin, J. A. "Culture, Consumption, and Adult Education: Refashioning Consumer Education for Adults as a Political Site Using a Cultural Studies Framework." *Adult Education Quarterly,* 2005a, *55*(3), 165–181.

Sandlin, J. A. "'Spend Smart, Live Rich'? A Critical Analysis of the Consumer Education Lifestyle Magazine *Budget Living* and Its Readers' Forums." In R. Hill and R. Kiely (eds.), *Proceedings of the 46th Annual Adult Education Research Conference.* Athens: University of Georgia, 2005b.

Solorzano, D. G., and Delgado Bernal, D. "Examining Transformational Resistance Through a Critical Race and Latcrit Theory Framework." *Urban Education,* 2001, *36*(3), 308–342.

Storey, J. *Cultural Consumption and Everyday Life: Cultural Studies in Practice.* New York: Oxford University Press, 1999.

Storey, J. *Cultural Theory and Popular Culture.* (4th ed.) Athens: University of Georgia Press, 2006.

Tisdell, E. J., and Thompson, P. M. "*Crash*-ing into Pop Culture in Dealing with Diversity: Adult Education and Critical Media Literacy About Movies and Television." In M. Hagen and E. Goff (eds.), *Proceedings of the 47th Annual Adult Education Research Conference.* Minneapolis: University of Minnesota, 2006.

Usher, R., Bryant, I., and Johnston, R. *Adult Education and the Postmodern Challenge.* New York: Routledge, 1997.

Williams, R. "Base and Superstructure in Marxist Cultural Theory." *New Left Review,* 1973, *82,* 3–16.

Wright, R. R. "A Different Definition of 'Boob-Tube': What Dr. Catherine Gale, of *The Avengers,* Taught Women." In M. Hagen and E. Goff (eds.), *Proceedings of the 47th Annual Adult Education Research Conference.* Minneapolis: University of Minnesota, 2006.

JENNIFER A. SANDLIN is assistant professor in the Division of Curriculum and Instruction at Arizona State University, Tempe.

9

This chapter summarizes the main themes in this volume: the role of popular culture and entertainment media in facilitating critical media literacy with adult learners; the influence of popular culture on our understanding of ourselves and others; and the ways in which popular culture reinforces or resists the dominant culture.

The Influence of Popular Culture and Entertainment Media on Adult Education

Patricia M. Thompson

While visiting the Air and Space Museum in Washington, D.C., with my ten- and eleven-year-old sons, I asked the boys whether they knew who Goddard, the father of space travel, was. My oldest son replied, "Oh, he is Jimmy Neutron's dog!" Because I was studying the influence of popular culture and entertainment media on adults at the time, my son's reply reinforced my observation that not only are adults influenced by current popular culture but they have knowledge that has been acquired and constructed through immersion in popular culture and entertainment media from the time they were small children.

Recognizing the influence of popular culture in our own lives is the first step to harnessing its educational potential. Ray Browne (2005), the co-founder of the Popular Culture Association and the founder of the American Cultural Association, argues that the most significant academic and cultural development in the latter half of the twentieth century was the "rerecognition" of the importance of understanding popular culture. He posits that students and teachers are immersed in the culture that surrounds them and that popular culture is "a kind of daily world currency" that cannot and should not be kept from the academic sphere, "no matter how hermetically tight our minds our sealed" (p. 3).

Despite criticism that the content of the mass media and popular culture is mind numbing or destructive of the moral landscape of society,

NEW DIRECTIONS FOR ADULT AND CONTINUING EDUCATION, no. 115, Fall 2007 © 2007 Wiley Periodicals, Inc.
Published online in Wiley InterScience (www.interscience.wiley.com) • DOI: 10.1002/ace.270

Steven Johnson (2006), a popular science author, proposes that pop culture is becoming increasingly sophisticated and intellectually demanding. He argues that television shows now have complex, interwoven story lines that need to be followed weekly. Technology such as dvds, videos, and on-demand programming allows the consumer not only to be entertained by television shows and films but to stop and start them and thus to dissect, analyze, and learn from them. Many people have disagreed with Johnson, but his book has sparked discussion, especially on the internet. Our hope for this volume is that the authors' contributions will similarly spark discussion, debate, and new ways of thinking about the relationship between popular culture and entertainment media and learning.

I have to be honest. Prior to my involvement in doing research on and teaching about popular culture and entertainment media, I did not give these topics much thought. I did not watch a lot of television and rarely had time to see a movie at the theater; when I rented movies to watch at home, I frequently fell asleep! As an educator, I often incorporated clips from movies and television shows to connect with learners. But I rarely evaluated the unintended messages students were receiving from the media I chose, especially their portrayals of gender, race, age, and sexual orientation.

After more than two years of researching the subject and reading, teaching, and writing about it, I have changed personally and profession-ally. Now, I find it difficult not to analyze media or to think about how the media influence my learning and the learning of the adults I teach. Not only do I propose that educators need to understand and embrace critical media literacy, but I also incorporate it into my life and use it to evaluate my own media consumption.

This chapter reviews the three major themes of this volume: promoting critical media literacy and using entertainment media to connect with learn-ers; using popular culture and entertainment media to understand ourselves and others; and recognizing and understanding how popular culture and entertainment media both reinforce and resist the dominant culture.

Promoting Critical Media Literacy

Integrating popular culture and entertainment media in adult education settings is an easy way to connect with learners and have them connect with each other; doing so can also promote critical media literacy. As Elizabeth J. Tisdell noted in Chapter One, there are many definitions of critical media literacy. Alvermann and Hagood (2000) define it broadly as "helping students experience the pleasures of popular culture while simultaneously uncovering the codes and practices that work to silence or disempower them as readers, viewers and learners in general" (p. 194). The authors of the chapters in this volume described the different ways they develop critical media literacy as Alvermann and Hagood define it and the different ways they draw on popular culture and entertainment media to connect with learners. I offer a few examples here.

New Directions for Adult and Continuing Education • DOI: 10.1002/ace

In Chapter Six, Barbara P. Heuer discussed the relationships among literacy, literacy education, popular culture, and entertainment media and described how she has used popular culture to connect with learners. She also highlighted a study that found that adults with low literacy skills draw on media of many types and apply the information they gain in their daily lives. Heuer encouraged us to think about how we define literacy in order to recognize the importance of critical media literacy, especially for literacy educators. Explaining that "literacy is the ability to make meaning from and to interpret resources and relationships in one's environment," she used this broad definition to suggest that literacy educators consider the influence of popular culture and entertainment media on their students. Even though a student may not have the ability to read text or compute numbers very well, he or she has the ability to learn informally through various media venues. Heuer emphasized that literacy educators need to recognize the functional, liberal, and radical/critical perspectives of literacy, which support seeing students' daily practices and interactions with media as part of literacy.

In Chapter Five Maxwell A. Fink and Deborah C. Foote discussed how they use *The Simpsons* not only to connect with students but to encourage students to think critically about the world around them. They suggest that "*The Simpsons* can go beyond its extremely entertaining two-dimensional depictions to address critical and sophisticated issues often introduced and presented in the college classroom." Both authors incorporate the show in their teaching practices in the humanities in different ways. Because of the cultural and satirical nature of the show they are able to use it to teach students to critically assess the media and to critically assess their world.

Heather Stuckey and Kelly Kring, in Chapter Three, shared their experiences of using popular film in a course offered to promote educators' critical media literacy. I was one of the colleagues who team-taught this course with Stuckey, and Tisdell was the other. It was an invaluable learning experience for each of us, as well as for our students. As I read Stuckey's and Kring's descriptions of their experiences and reflected on mine and those of other students in the class, I found the disparate interests and insights amazing.

Stuckey was focused on semiotics and how those who create media use signs and symbols to convey messages. She had the students critically analyze and interpret the messages presented in the signs and symbols that pervade entertainment media. In Chapter Two, Talmadge C. Guy described the messages and assumptions behind a billboard he saw with a blond, buxom woman promoting the use of generators. Stuckey's interest and expertise in semiotics enhanced students' learning by teaching them how to attend to messages such as that one. In this course I was interested in how the students identified with characters in the entertainment media, how they analyzed the characters, and how they incorporated critical media literacy into their educational practice. While Stuckey was asking students to look beyond the surface and to analyze the messages behind the images,

I was asking them to reflect on their relationship to the characters, the relationships among the characters themselves, and how these relationships reflect or challenge societal norms.

The students in the class had their own reasons for enrolling in the course. We found it challenging, and at times frustrating, when students became so involved with the pleasure associated with the media that, despite our constant prodding, they forgot to analyze their experience! As educators we had to heed the advice of Julie Hamston (2002), who suggests that teachers should recognize that much of the learning that occurs from engaging with the media is "bound up with the pleasure that it gives" (p. 108).

Let's face it, most adults watch television or go to see a movie to be entertained or because they make it a social event with friends or family members. I have not met many people who say, "Oh, tonight *Desperate Housewives* is on TV. I can't wait to analyze how this evening's episode is reinforcing and resisting the dominant discourse of society!" If we are going to encourage students to analyze entertainment media, we also should try to understand the factors that make entertainment media pleasurable in the first place.

While encouraging learners to be critical consumers, we have to recognize "the potential 'unpleasure' of critical literacy, where critique is seen as largely negative and a practice of deconstruction only" (Hamston, 2002, p. 108). When learners begin to analyze the media, their viewing choices often change. One student in class stated that she could no longer watch her favorite show because she sees it differently now that she has analyzed it from a critical perspective.

It is important to reinforce Guy's approach to using critical media literacy in his own practice. As he explained in Chapter Two, "I have found it important to avoid imposing my analysis on students. Sometimes students have different interpretations of the pop-culture examples that I use." As educators we want to challenge students to challenge themselves to critically assess media and their interpretations of it, while respecting their individuality and understanding how their backgrounds, life experiences, ages, and sociocultural contexts may influence their interpretations.

Mary Stone Hanley made this point clearly in Chapter Four when discussing the influence of hip hop on "rising generations." In order to become a better educator, Hanley entered a world that most people of her generation tend to disregard or criticize and that most of us in education criticize for its misogynist, violent messages. Hanley, however, found in hip hop culture a hotbed of rich creative processes in which teens and young adults show their talent and thoughtfulness as they express their feelings and ideas. Not only did she learn about this world, but she encouraged those who work with youth and younger adults to experience hip hop and the transformations that it can facilitate, as well as to understand the cultural context in which it developed. The use of hip hop also can promote the development of critical media literacy, as well as creativity and engagement.

New Directions for Adult and Continuing Education • DOI: 10.1002/ace

Understanding Ourselves and Others

In Chapter One, Tisdell highlighted a study that she and I did together (Tisdell and Thompson, 2007). In it we explored how adult learners and educators of adults, as a result of their engagement with popular culture, construct knowledge based on gender, race, and sexual orientation. A main finding was that the participants chose media that gave them a way to find alternative narratives in their own lives. Their favorite characters were those whom they related to, whom they wanted to be like, or who helped them understand themselves or people who were different from them in some way.

Many of the other authors also took up this theme. For example, in Chapter Two, Guy provided wonderful illustrations from his educational practice of popular culture both informing and challenging beliefs and understandings, especially in the areas of gender, race, and class. Rather than seeing popular culture as "an imposition of the dominant culture on the marginalized," he understands it to be "a complex interplay of cultural products and meanings placed in circulation by differently positioned persons." He suggested that people both receive these messages and act on them. He went on to discuss the influence of popular culture in our contemporary lives, arguing that it provides avenues whereby people can reconstruct their own identities and understand how others with different positionalities have constructed different identities.

As I mentioned previously, I am not a big movie-goer. But I did see the movie *Dreamgirls* with a friend who is African American and who grew up in the segregated South. Throughout the movie, I was intrigued by how differently we reacted to the various scenes and messages. For example, I had never heard of the chitlin circuit. But, for her, an avid music fan, the chitlin circuit was common knowledge. When we shared our perspectives and interpretations afterward, I had an opportunity to hear about a part of her that is often hidden from those in my predominantly white, middle-class world.

The idea of identity construction, or (re)construction, took another form in Chapter Seven. Robin Redmon Wright shared her research on the influence on young women of an action drama that was popular in Britain in the 1960s. For the participants in her study and other women who lived in Britain and experienced Honor Blackman's character, Cathy Gale, in *The Avengers,* the focus was less on understanding others and more on empowering women to understand themselves and their potential. Unlike the women in contemporary advertisements, whom Guy discussed in Chapter Two, Gale was the antithesis of the feminine archetype, especially at the time. As a result, many British women of that era saw her as a role model or an inspiration. When Wright interviewed these women nearly thirty years later, she recognized the power of Gale as a role model. In her chapter in this volume Wright argued that educators need to understand the popular culture in which their students live and learn and how it affects their lives. "We prove by our breadth of knowledge that educators of adults do, indeed, know about the world our students inhabit and that we can connect to it—no matter what our age." As educators, we need to recognize the power that popular culture and entertainment media have in order to meet students where they live.

Fink and Foote highlighted this need in Chapter Five, where they described both how they relate to *The Simpsons* as Gen Xers themselves and how they use the show in their classes. Because the show has been an influence on popular culture for such a long time, most Gen Xers and Gen Yers have grown up knowing and often identifying with Bart, Lisa, Maggie, Homer, and Marge. Fink matched the themes and messages of *The Simpsons* to the values often imputed to Gen Xers. He explains, "I can see clearly now how the traits that qualify me as a Gen Xer are the same qualities that make me such a huge fan of *The Simpsons* and an even bigger fan of the critical mind-set inspired by the show since the dawn of that generational era."

In this way pop culture and especially entertainment media such as television and cinema can imprint and affect our core values. I remember, as a young girl, watching *The Sound of Music* every year on television. Long before I knew much about World War II or Nazi Germany, my visceral response to a swastika was negative. How many other messages from entertainment media have molded and continue to mold my value system in ways that I do not even recognize? This is the reason educators need to critically analyze media and to develop critical media literacy.

A good example of the need for critical media literacy was given in Chapter Three, where Kring described the knowledge she gained from analyzing her favorite movie, *The Way We Were*. Her initial appreciation of the movie stemmed from the romantic relationship depicted in it. But as she began to critically analyze the film, she learned about the political aspects. She researched that time in history and discovered the effect that blacklisting and McCarthyism had on the entertainment world. As a result she gained a whole new understanding of the film.

Reinforcing and Resisting the Dominant Culture

Often media reinforce the images and values of the dominant culture (Giroux, 2002). As the authors in this volume have suggested, pop culture and entertainment media are created for the cultural mainstream, and so most entertainment media, especially television, reproduce traditional values and norms. But entertainment media can also challenge or resist the dominant culture, as was seen in Wright's report in Chapter Seven on the impact of Cathy Gale on women's views of themselves and of gender.

Most media both reproduce and resist culture. One example is given in Stuckey and Kring's discussion in Chapter Three of the movie *Brokeback Mountain*. As they mentioned, even though the film revolved around the homosexual love relationship between the two main characters, much of the movie, such as the love scenes with their wives, reinforced the values of the dominant culture.

A prominent theme in Chapter Five was how *The Simpsons* presents an "oppositional culture" despite being part of mainstream culture. Although Fink and Foote recognize that the show is to Gen Xers what *Leave It to Beaver* was to the boomers, they point out that the show uses satire to challenge mainstream ideals by "constantly shifting perspective; it makes fun of one social group while winking at another, and then may reverse that approach later on."

Hanley's depiction, in Chapter Four, of hip hop as a way for black youth "to construct a culture of language, behaviors, relationships, and commodities that counter the dominant discourse in schools and middle-class white communities on multiple levels" is a strong example of how popular culture can resist the dominant discourse. However, although hip hop artists counter the dominant culture, they also reinforce it by, as Guy pointed out in Chapter Two, representing black women in "negative and misogynistic ways."

In Chapter Eight, Jennifer A. Sandlin introduced the concept of cultural resistance and described how popular culture and its message of consumerism are being challenged in alternative media spaces. Through her research on consumerism and consumption, Sandlin recognized the impact of popular culture on society; "popular culture is always at once a site of hegemonic power and of political resistance. "As Guy reported in Chapter Two, the intent of media-fashioned popular culture is to "exploit consumer desire in order to promote profit," but cultural resistance challenges this dominant discourse. Sandlin discussed how culture jamming, a form of cultural resistance, works as critical adult education, and she emphasized the importance of paying attention to informal sites of learning. She illustrated how groups such as Adbusters Media Foundation and Reverend Billy and his Church of Stop Shopping provide media spaces in which anticonsumption activists can campaign.

This constant pull and push of the media creates a dynamic interplay for educators and learners to analyze and critique. Guy suggested in Chapter Two that when we look at media and popular culture through a critical lens, we can become cynical. But, as mentioned previously, most individuals use entertainment media for pleasure. Becoming critical consumers of media takes conscious effort. As a society, we are enamored of popular culture and shaped by it; but we also can shape it.

Conclusions

The idea that popular culture and entertainment media influence us in both conscious and unconscious ways is not new. In Chapter Six, Heuer quotes the sociologist David Riesman's work from over fifty years ago; he suggested, even then, that the media influence individuals. Since that time, popular culture has evolved, reflecting and devising the signs of the times. The use of alternative spaces, such as internet sites, for creating entertainment will continue to influence society and challenge educators. The importance of the internet was reflected in *Time* magazine's choosing YOU (meaning the general public) as Person of the Year for 2006. *Time* boldly stated that "you control the media now, and the world will never be the same" (Grossman, 2006/2007, p. 42); in doing so it recognized that technology has created a platform for individuals to express themselves in ways that people a generation ago could not have even imagined.

An excellent example is the internet site YouTube. *Time* reported that "users upload 65,000 new videos to the site every day. A year ago, they [YouTube™ subscribers] watched 10 million videos a day; now they watch 100 million" (Cloud, 2006/2007, p. 70). Also, YouTube has purchased the rights to various vintage television shows, such as *Gumby* (*Today Show*, Feb. 13, 2007). Now, with the click of a mouse, you can watch, analyze, and critique entertainment media that have influenced multiple generations across the globe.

These new spaces provide opportunities for cultural resistance, as Sandlin suggested in Chapter Eight. But, as with traditional media, we need to view these spaces with a critical eye, especially as they gain popularity and advertising dollars. We also need to ask, Who has the access, knowledge, and skills necessary to be the "you"s who shape the media? Whose voices are not being heard? How will this interactive medium influence individuals and society? The answers lie in the future.

References

Alvermann, D. E., and Hagood, M. C. "Critical Media Literacy: Research, Theory, and Practice in 'New Times.'" *Journal of Educational Research*, 2000, 93(3), 193–205.

Browne, R. *Popular Culture Studies Across the Curriculum*. Jefferson, N.C.: McFarland, 2005.

Cloud, J. "The YouTube Gurus: How a Couple of Regular Guys Built a Company That Changed the Way We See Ourselves." *Time*, Dec. 25, 2006/Jan. 1, 2007, pp. 66–74.

Giroux, H. *Breaking into the Movies: Film and the Culture of Politics*. New York: Blackwell, 2002.

Grossman, L. "Power to the People." *Time*, Dec. 25, 2006/Jan. 1, 2007, pp. 42–56.

Hamston, J. "Pleasurable Texts: Popular Culture in the Classroom." *Screen Education*, 2002, 37, 107–112.

Johnson, S. *Everything Bad Is Good for You: How Today's Popular Culture Is Actually Making Us Smarter*. New York: Penguin Books, 2006.

Tisdell, E. J., and Thompson, P. M. "Seeing 'From a Different Angle': The Role of Pop Culture in Teaching for Diversity and Critical Media Literacy in Adult Education." *International Journal of Lifelong Education*, forthcoming, 26(6).

PATRICIA M. THOMPSON *is a doctoral student in adult education at the Pennsylvania State University, Harrisburg, and currently works as the editorial associate for the* Adult Education Quarterly.

INDEX

Adult-literacy learners: animation and graphics for, 58; deficit model, 57, 61; mass media use by, 56

Adult educators: connection to learning outside classroom, 68–69; consumers of popular culture, 7–8; critique of pop culture by, 22; drawing on popular culture, 10–11; popular music and, 35; use of popular culture by, 69–70

Adult learner: competition and, 59; context and culture of, 58; media-usage habits of, 60

Adult learning: culture jamming as site of, 76; détournement, 79–80; pedagogical hinge of culture jamming and, 79–80; predominant forms of, 56; student-centered principles, 58

Adult literacy, surveys of, 56

Adult literacy media alliance, tv411, 58

Adult literacy programs, main focus of, 57

Adults with limited literacy skills, media-use habits of, 56

Advertising. *See also* Commercials: profit motive of, 17; representation of women in, 18–19

African american youth, music and, 36

American family, popular conception of, 49

Animation: for adult-literacy learners, 58; intimidation factor and, 51; representation of behavior in, 51

Art experience, cognition and emotion in, 38

Assumptions by critical media-literacy scholars, critical medial literacy theory and, 9

Australia, critical media literacy, 7

Banking method of teaching, open-mic as alternative form to, 42

Bias in television, media literacy and, 7

Black popular music, importance to black youth, 36

Black women, popular culture and, 18

British gender roles, traditional, 64

Brokeback Mountain, movie: interpretation of images in, 30; sexual orientation and, 29–30

Brown, D., *Da Vinci Code,* 5

Buffy the Vampire Slayer, television show, 7

Canada, critical media literacy, 7

Carnival, medieval: defined, 48; *Simpsons as, 48*

Characters in movies, identification with, 25

Christianity, critique of, in *simpsons, 47*

Class perspective, reading cultural images from, 7

Coding practice, in critique of popular culture, 21

Cognition, art experience and, 38

Cognitive prototypes, of black people, 18

Commander in Chief, television series, gender representation in, 20

Commercials, selling sex through, 19

Community college, use of *Simpsons, 51*

Competition, in adult learners, 59

Confrontation, character of Cathy Gale in *Avengers, 67*

Construction of meaning, critical media literacy theory and, 9

Consumerism, adult learning and education and, 73

Consumption, adult learning and education and, 73

Crash, movie, 16

Crash, movie, cultural dynamics portrayed in, 20

Creation of art: hip hop forms, 40–42; learning about students through, 41

Creative process, sharing culture through, 42

Creative symbolism, used by black youth, 38

Creativity, hip hop and, 38

Critical adult education: anticonsumption social movements and, 74; culture jamming as, 73–81

Critical analysis: framework for, 21–22; of hip hop, 38; imposition of analysis on students, 20–21; of movies, 28; of pop culture, 19–22

Critical commentary, television and, 68

Critical literacy, opportunities in hip hop, 40

policy can make space for the emergence of difference related to sexual orientation and gender identity.
ISBN 078799495-2

ACE111 Authenticity in Teaching

Patricia Cranton

Authenticity is one of those concepts, like soul, spirit, or imagination, that are easier to define in terms of what they are not than what they are. We can fairly easily say that someone who lies to students or who pretends to know things he or she does not know or who deliberately dons a teaching persona is not authentic. But do the opposite behaviors guarantee authentic teaching? Not necessarily. Becoming an authentic teacher appears to be a developmental process that relies on experience, maturity, self-exploration, and reflection. It is the purpose of this volume to explore a variety of ways of thinking about authenticity in teaching, from the perspective of scholars who dedicate themselves to understanding adult education theory and research and from that of practitioners who see themselves as working toward authentic practice.

The contributors address five overlapping and interrelated dimensions of authenticity: self-awareness and self-exploration; awareness of others (especially students); relationships with students; awareness of cultural, social, and educational contexts and their influence on practice; and critical self-reflection on teaching.
ISBN 0-7879-9403-0

ACE110 The Neuroscience of Adult Learning

Sandra Johnson and Kathleen Taylor

Recent research developments have added much to our understanding of brain function. Though some neurobiologists have explored implications for learning, few have focused on learning in adulthood. This issue of New Directions for Adult and Continuing Education, *The Neuroscience of Adult Learning,* examines links between this emerging research and adult educators' practice. Now that it is possible to trace the pathways of the brain involved in various learning tasks, we can also explore which learning environments are likely to be most effective. Volume contributors include neurobiologists, educators, and clinical psychologists who have illuminated connections between how the brain functions and how to enhance learning. Among the topics explored here are basic brain architecture and "executive" functions of the brain, how learning can "repair" the effects of psychological trauma on the brain, effects of stress and emotions on learning, the centrality of experience to learning and construction of knowledge, the mentor-learner relationship, and intersections between best practices in adult learning and current neurobiological discoveries. Although the immediate goal of this volume is to expand the discourse on teaching and learning practices, our overarching goal is to encourage adult learners toward more complex ways of knowing.
ISBN 0-7879-8704-2

ACE109 Teaching for Change: Fostering Transformative Learning in the Classroom

Edward W. Taylor

Fostering transformative learning is about teaching for change. It is not an approach to be taken lightly, arbitrarily, or without much thought. Many would argue that it requires intentional action, a willingness to take personal risk, a genuine concern for the learners' betterment, and the wherewithal to draw on a variety of methods and techniques that help create a classroom

environment that encourages and supports personal growth. What makes the work of transformative learning even more difficult is the lack of clear signposts or guidelines that teachers can follow when they try to teach for change. There is now a need to return to the classroom and look through the lens of those who have been engaged in the practice of fostering transformative learning. This volume's authors are seasoned practitioners and scholars who have grappled with the fundamental issues associated with teaching for change (emotion, expressive ways of knowing, power, cultural difference, context, teacher authenticity, spirituality) in a formal classroom setting; introduced innovations that enhance the practice of fostering transformative learning; and asked ethical questions that need to be explored and reflected upon when practicing transformative learning in the classroom.
ISBN 0-7879-8584-8

ACE108 Adulthood: New Terrain
Mary Alice Wolf
One of the many surprises about the lifespan perspective is that individuals, families, institutions, and corporations lead *many* lives. The purpose of this resource is to acquaint and update practitioners in adult education and related roles with emerging and creative methods of 1) appreciating the learner's perspective, 2) moderating content and learning format to enhance meaning-making in the learning environment, and 3) developing tools to address alternative modes of development and growth that occur in adulthood and challenge adult educators on a daily basis.

What does the new adult learner look like? This volume contains theory and research on learners who turn to educational programs in times of transition and explores ways of connecting with new cognitive and affective meanings.

This volume explores dimensions of adult development from ethnographic, research, and theoretical perspectives. It addresses adult learners' experience and meaning of education as an ongoing resource for well-being and positive development across the lifecourse. It updates the reader in the emerging terrain of adulthood; adult learning philosophies are implemented and modified to meet adults' developmental mandate to continue learning in order to make meaning and find purpose during the countless transitions of the ever-increasing adult years.
ISBN 0-7879-8396-0

ACE107 Artistic Ways of Knowing: Expanded Opportunities for Teaching and Learning
Randee Lipson Lawrence
This volume of *New Directions for Adult and Continuing Education* challenges the dominant paradigm of how knowledge is typically constructed and shared in adult education settings by focusing on ways in which adult educators can expand learning opportunities and experiences for their learners. Art appeals universally to us all and has the capacity to bridge cultural differences. Art can also foster individual and social transformation, promoting dialogue and deepening awareness of ourselves and the world around us. The contributors to this volume include actors, musicians, photographers, storytellers, and poets, all of whom also happen to be adult educators. In each chapter, the author describes how one or more forms of artistic expression were used to promote learning in formal or informal adult education settings. In each case, the purpose of education was not to teach

art (that is, not to develop expertise in acting, poetry writing, or creating great works of art). Conversely, art was used as a means to access learning in subjects as divergent as English language acquisition, action research, community awareness, and social justice.
ISBN 0-7879-8284-9

ACE106 Class Concerns: Adult Education and Social Class

Tom Nesbitt

This volume of *New Directions for Adult and Continuing Education* brings together several leading progressive adult educators to explore how class affects different arenas of adult education practice and discourse. It highlights the links between adult education, the material and social conditions of daily and working lives, and the economic and political systems that underpin them. Chapters focus on adult education policies; teaching; learning and identity formation; educational institutions and social movements; and the relationships between class, gender, and race. Overall, the volume reaffirms the salience of class in shaping the lives we lead and the educational approaches we develop. It offers suggestions for adult educators to identify and resist the encroachments of global capitalism and understand the role of education in promoting social equality. Finally, it suggests that a class perspective can provide an antidote to much of the social amnesia, self-absorption, and apolitical theorizing that pervades current adult education discourse.
ISBN 0-7879-8128-1

ACE105 HIV/AIDS Education for Adults

John P. Egan

Contributors from the United States, Canada, and Australia, working in university-based and community-based environments and for divergent communities—present specific experiences in the fight against HIV/AIDS. They share stories of shifting paradigms and challenging norms, and of seeking and finding innovation. Topics examined include the struggle for meaning and power in HIV/AIDS education, HIV prevention workers and injection drug users, community-based research, grassroots response to HIV/AIDS in Nova Scotia, sex workers and HIV/AIDS education, and the Tuskegee Syphilis Study and legacy recruitment for experimental vaccines. By examining HIV/AIDS through an adult education lens, we gain insights into how communities (and governments) can respond quickly and effectively to emergent health issues—and other issues linked to marginalization.
ISBN 0-7879-8032-3

ACE104 Embracing and Enhancing the Margins of Adult Education

Meg Wise, Michelle Glowacki-Dudka

Adult educators increasingly risk and resist being placed at the margins of academic and other organizations. This volume argues that depending on how those margins are defined, margins can be a place of creativity and power from which to examine and challenge dominant ideology and practice. Chapters explore advances and effective practices being made in the margins of adult education from several perspectives including community-based programs, interreligious learning, human resource development, African American underrepresentation in the academy, and degree-granting adult education programs. Other areas explored include an interdisciplinary Web-based patient education research program and educational focus on citizenship and public responsibility skills.
ISBN 0-7879-7859-0

NEW DIRECTIONS FOR ADULT & CONTINUING EDUCATION
Order Form
SUBSCRIPTIONS AND SINGLE ISSUES

DISCOUNTED BACK ISSUES:

Use this form to receive **20% off** *all back issues of New Directions for Adult & Continuing Education. All single issues priced at* **$23.20** *(normally $29.00)*

TITLE   ISSUE NO.   ISBN

_____   _____   _____

_____   _____   _____

_____   _____   _____

Call **888-378-2537** *or see mailing instructions below. When calling, mention the promotional code, JB7ND, to receive your discount.*

SUBSCRIPTIONS: *(1 year, 4 issues)*

☐ New Order   ☐ Renewal

U.S.	☐ Individual: $80	☐ Institutional: $195
Canada/Mexico	☐ Individual: $80	☐ Institutional: $235
All Others	☐ Individual: $104	☐ Institutional: $269

Call **888-378-2537** *or see mailing and pricing instructions below. Online subscriptions are available at www.interscience.wiley.com.*

Copy or detach page and send to:
   John Wiley & Sons, Journals Dept, 5th Floor
   989 Market Street, San Francisco, CA 94103-1741

Order Form can also be faxed to: 888-481-2665

Issue/Subscription Amount: $ _____	**SHIPPING CHARGES:**		
Shipping Amount: $ _____	SURFACE	Domestic	Canadian
(for single issues only—subscription prices include shipping)	First Item	$5.00	$6.00
Total Amount: $ _____	Each Add'l Item	$3.00	$1.50

(No sales tax for U.S. subscriptions. Canadian residents, add GST for subscription orders. Individual rate subscriptions must be paid by personal check or credit card. Individual rate subscriptions may not be resold as library copies.)

☐ Payment enclosed (U.S. check or money order only. All payments must be in U.S. dollars.)

☐ VISA ☐ MC ☐ Amex # _____ Exp. Date _____

Card Holder Name _____ Card Issue # _____

Signature _____ Day Phone _____

☐ Bill Me (U.S. institutional orders only. Purchase order required.)

Purchase order # _____
                 Federal Tax ID13559302   GST 89102 8052

Name _____

Address _____

Phone _____ E-mail _____

BICENTENNIAL
1807
(W)WILEY
2007
BICENTENNIAL

THE WILEY BICENTENNIAL–KNOWLEDGE FOR GENERATIONS

*E*ach generation has its unique needs and aspirations. When Charles Wiley first opened his small printing shop in lower Manhattan in 1807, it was a generation of boundless potential searching for an identity. And we were there, helping to define a new American literary tradition. Over half a century later, in the midst of the Second Industrial Revolution, it was a generation focused on building the future. Once again, we were there, supplying the critical scientific, technical, and engineering knowledge that helped frame the world. Throughout the 20th Century, and into the new millennium, nations began to reach out beyond their own borders and a new international community was born. Wiley was there, expanding its operations around the world to enable a global exchange of ideas, opinions, and know-how.

For 200 years, Wiley has been an integral part of each generation's journey, enabling the flow of information and understanding necessary to meet their needs and fulfill their aspirations. Today, bold new technologies are changing the way we live and learn. Wiley will be there, providing you the must-have knowledge you need to imagine new worlds, new possibilities, and new opportunities.

Generations come and go, but you can always count on Wiley to provide you the knowledge you need, when and where you need it!

WILLIAM J. PESCE
PRESIDENT AND CHIEF EXECUTIVE OFFICER

PETER BOOTH WILEY
CHAIRMAN OF THE BOARD